CIPS STUDY MATTERS

ADVANCED CERTIFICATE
IN PROCUREMENT AND SUPPLY OPERATIONS

COURSE BOOK

Procurement and supply relationships

Printed and distributed by:

The Chartered Institute of Purchasing & Supply, Easton House, Easton on the Hill, Stamford, Lincolnshire
PE9 3NZ
Tel: +44 (0) 1780 756 777
Fax: +44 (0) 1780 751 610
Email: info@cips.org
Website: www.cips.org

First edition September 2012

Contents

Preface

Welcome to your new Course Book.

Your Course Book provides detailed coverage of all topics specified in the unit content.

For a full explanation of how to use your new Course Book, turn now to page ix. And good luck in your studies!

A note on style

Throughout your Course Books you will find that we use the masculine form of personal pronouns. This convention is adopted purely for the sake of stylistic convenience – we just don't like saying 'he/she' all the time. Please don't think this reflects any kind of bias or prejudice.

September 2012

Procurement and Supply Relationships

The Unit Content

The unit content is reproduced below, together with reference to the chapter in this Course Book where each topic is covered.

Unit characteristics

On completion of this unit, candidates will be able to explain a range of main principles and techniques that help develop customer and supplier relationships. It is essential for procurement and supply personnel to form effective relationships with suppliers, internal and external customers and other stakeholders.

This unit introduces the principles of marketing, the importance of cross-functional working and the need to communicate effectively both within the organisation and with people from external organisations.

Learning outcomes, assessment criteria and indicative content

Chapter

1.0 Understand the range of both internal and external relationships in procurement and supply

1.1 Assess the roles of personnel within an organisation who may be involved in a relationship in procurement and supply

- Procurement and supply and its interactions with other functions   1
- Devolved purchasers   1
- The decision making unit (organisational buying behaviour)   1
- Account management   1

1.2 Classify the stakeholders in a relationship between purchasers and suppliers

- Defining stakeholders   2
- Classifying internal and external stakeholders   2
- The RACI (responsible, accountable, consulted, informed) model as a classification tool   2
- Communicating with stakeholders   2

1.3 Explain the appropriateness of cross-functional working when making relationships in procurement and supply

- Forming cross-functional teams   3
- The added value procurement and supply provides to cross-functional working and internal marketing   3
- Barriers to teamworking   3
- Stages of team formation   3
- Characteristics of successful teams   3

How to Use Your Course Book

Organising your study

'Organising' is the key word: unless you are a very exceptional student, you will find a haphazard approach is insufficient, particularly if you are having to combine study with the demands of a full-time job.

A good starting point is to timetable your studies, in broad terms, between now and the date of your assessment. How many units are you attempting? How many chapters are there in the Course Book for each subject? Now do the sums: how many days/weeks do you have for each chapter to be studied?

Remember:

- Not every week can be regarded as a study week – you may be going on holiday, for example, or there may be weeks when the demands of your job are particularly heavy. If these can be foreseen, you should allow for them in your timetabling.
- You also need a period leading up to the assessment in which you will revise and practise what you have learned.

Once you have done the calculations, make a week-by-week timetable for yourself for each paper, allowing for study and revision of the entire unit content between now and the date of the assessment.

Getting started

Aim to find a quiet and undisturbed location for your study, and plan as far as possible to use the same period each day. Getting into a routine helps avoid wasting time. Make sure you have all the materials you need before you begin – keep interruptions to a minimum.

Using the Course Book

You should refer to the Course Book to the extent that you need it.

- If you are a newcomer to the subject, you will probably need to read through the Course Book quite thoroughly. This will be the case for most students.
- If some areas are already familiar to you – either through earlier studies or through your practical work experience – you may choose to skip sections of the Course Book.

The content of the Course Book

This Course Book has been designed to give detailed coverage of every topic in the unit content. As you will see from pages vii–viii, each topic mentioned in the unit content is dealt with in a chapter of the Course Book. For the most part the order of the Course Book follows the order of the unit content closely, though departures from this principle have occasionally been made in the interest of a logical learning order.

Each chapter begins with a reference to the assessment criteria and indicative content to be covered in the chapter. Each chapter is divided into sections, listed in the introduction to the chapter, and for the most part being actual captions from the unit content.

All of this enables you to monitor your progress through the unit content very easily and provides reassurance that you are tackling every subject that is assessable.

Each chapter contains the following features.

- Clear coverage of each topic in a concise and approachable format
- A chapter summary
- Self-test questions

The study phase

For each chapter you should begin by glancing at the main headings (listed at the start of the chapter). Then read fairly rapidly through the body of the text to absorb the main points. If it's there in the text, you can be sure it's there for a reason, so try not to skip unless the topic is one you are familiar with already.

Then return to the beginning of the chapter to start a more careful reading. You may want to take brief notes as you go along.

Test your recall and understanding of the material by attempting the self-test questions. These are accompanied by cross-references to paragraphs where you can check your answers and refresh your memory.

The revision phase

Your approach to revision should be methodical and you should aim to tackle each main area of the unit content in turn. Re-read your notes. Then do some question practice. The CIPS website contains many past exam questions and you should aim to identify those that are suitable for the unit you are studying.

Additional reading

Your Course Book provides you with the key information needed for each module but CIPS strongly advocates reading as widely as possible to augment and reinforce your understanding. CIPS produces an official reading list of books, which can be downloaded from the bookshop area of the CIPS website.

To help you, we have identified one essential textbook for each subject. We recommend that you read this for additional information.

The essential textbook for this unit is *Purchasing and Supply Chain Management* by Kenneth Lysons and Brian Farrington.

CHAPTER 1

Procurement and Other Functions

Assessment criteria and indicative content

1.1 Assess the roles of personnel within an organisation who may be involved in a relationship in procurement and supply

- Procurement and supply and its interactions with other functions
- Devolved purchasers
- The decision making unit (organisational buying behaviour)
- Account management

Section headings

1. Interactions with other functions
2. Devolved purchasers
3. The decision making unit (DMU)
4. Account management

Introductory note

Organisational buying behaviour appears twice in the unit content: under Assessment Criteria 1.1 and 2.4. We take the view that in this chapter (covering 1.1) the emphasis should be on how the *marketer* views the topic, while in Chapter 8 (covering 2.4) we look at the topic from the perspective of the *purchaser*.

1   Interactions with other functions

Internal relationships

1.1   An organisation will try to satisfy the needs of an end user – the customer who wants to buy the organisation's products or services. However, it is rare for one organisation to satisfy the needs of an end user on its own, because the process – which may start with the production of raw materials and end with an over-the-counter sale in a retail shop – is too complex for any single organisation to cope with.

1.2   As a result, there are likely to be other organisations which are directly involved with specific aspects of the process. When we consider all of these organisations together we call them a supply chain. The supply chain and each of its elements is dedicated to meeting the needs of the end user although some of them may have no direct contact with that end user.

1.3   The supply chain can be seen as a long sequence of operations and activities, some of them carried out by the organisation itself, and some by suppliers or customers. Within an organisation, operations can be seen from an overall 'macro' perspective, as a single whole operation. It can also be seen as a number of separate operations that have to be carried out to transform the original inputs into the final finished output or service.

1.4   For example, an operation in an advertising agency to prepare a campaign for a client can be seen as a single overall operation, but it can also be seen as a number of 'micro operations', such as TV advertisement production, copy writing and copy editing for magazine advertisements, artwork design and production, media selection, media buying, and so on. Within each of these micro operations, there are other operations. Producing a TV advertisement, for example, involves micro operations such as story boarding and script writing, film production, the shooting of the film, film editing, and so on.

1.5   Each micro operation needs its input of resources, which might include both externally purchased materials and services and input from another department or work group in the organisation. Each micro operation is supplied both internally and externally.

1.6   The concept of internal supply leads on to the idea that within any organisation there are **internal suppliers** and **internal customers**.

1.7   For example, a road haulage company might have operational units for maintenance and servicing of vehicles, loading and driving. One micro process within the overall operation is the repair and servicing of vehicles. The mechanics servicing the vehicles are the internal supplier in the process, and the drivers of the vehicles are the internal customers. Similarly, the team that loads the vehicles is an internal supplier in the loading operation, and the drivers are again the internal customers.

1.8   In most respects, an internal customer should be treated as any external customer should be treated. The aim of the organisation should be to deliver a product or service that meets the customer's needs.

1.9   The main difference between an internal and an external customer is that in many cases, the internal customer has no freedom of choice of suppliers, and must use the internal supplier.

1.10   The concept of the internal customer is that within an organisation, internally delivered goods and services, as well as externally obtained goods and services, should meet the requirements and expectations of the internal customer. To do this, the needs of the internal customer have to be identified. The needs of the internal customer can only be properly established by having a dialogue with the customer.

1.11   Effective purchasing will therefore make use of cross-functional teams (CFTs), with representatives of the internal customers included within the team.

Internal customers of purchasing

1.12   Like all functions in an organisation, purchasing must be sensitive to the needs of customers. Purchasing staff must understand customer requirements because of their increasing strategic role in all aspects of organisational activities from product design onwards.

1.13   An extension of this basic idea is to regard each function in the organisation as having its own 'customers', who may be customers internal to the organisation, or who may be external to it. For example, purchasing staff may regard the production function as a 'customer', because the needs of production – for the right materials in the right place at the right time – must be met at least in part by efficient purchasing.

1.14 This attitude of treating other departments as customers encourages an effective, market-led approach to organising purchasing activities.

1.15 Too often in practice, the benefits of purchasing's involvement are resisted by internal users who are antagonised and alienated by their misconception of purchasing's role. In particular, they often believe that purchasing is solely concerned with the objective of low price, while ignoring other objectives legitimately pursued by user departments. This misconception must be overcome by a genuine philosophy of 'customer friendliness' among purchasing staff.

1.16 The value of this perspective on internal customers is that it encourages purchasing staff to plan proactively. Merely responding to requests from production (or other customer functions) as they arise is insufficient to ensure that internal customers are getting the service they require.

1.17 The primary roles of purchasing are as follows.

- To provide service to internal customers, such as production departments
- To reduce the costs incurred by the organisation
- To reduce the risks faced by the organisation
- To assist in quality issues, particularly in the early stages of product development
- To provide a satisfactory interface with other functions and with external customers

Setting internal objectives

1.18 To ensure that all of these roles are carried out satisfactorily (particularly the first and last ones), a logical approach is required to the organisation of the purchasing function. In particular, purchasing should not be a reactive function: work should be undertaken in line with agreed objectives and a predetermined strategy.

1.19 The objectives that may be identified for a purchasing function are very varied. They may include any or all of the following.

- To identify and select effective suppliers, and to manage relations with them in a constructive and profitable manner
- To protect the organisation's cost structure
- To ensure availability of required materials without undue stockholding costs
- To maintain constructive relationships with other organisational functions
- To ensure that value for money is obtained in managing the purchasing function

1.20 To attain these objectives, detailed plans capable of guiding day-to-day operational decisions must be made. These plans should cover such issues as:

- sourcing policy – single or multiple sourcing, or a combination depending on the materials concerned?
- make internally or source from outside?
- capture and analysis of purchasing-related information
- standardisation of products or emphasis on differentiation?
- links with other functional areas.

1.21 Once the plans are in place it is important to monitor their workings in practice. To what extent are they contributing to the objectives of purchasing and of the organisation as a whole? What changes might be made to improve the system?

1.22 Formalising the process of setting objectives and defining plans has great advantages. Above all, it imposes a discipline on purchasing functions which ensures that staff do not simply drift from one task to another without a clear sense of direction.

The status of purchasing in the organisation

1.23 Purchasing will achieve its maximum contribution to organisational goals only if its status in the organisation is sufficiently recognised. If the function is still seen primarily as providing administrative and clerical services, the opportunity to influence organisational achievement and delight internal customers will be severely limited.

1.24 Historically, the purchasing department has often been regarded as a support function, subordinated to production. This perception has gradually changed. Nowadays it is common in large organisations to find that the head of purchasing either reports directly to a main board director or is himself a director on the main board.

Who are the internal customers?

1.25 One of the prime purposes of a defined organisational structure is to ensure smooth liaison between different functions in order to achieve organisational objectives. Purchasing is just one example of this: links between purchasing and other functions are vital if purchasing itself is to perform to its optimum.

1.26 Purchasing's main internal customers, with whom it must establish and maintain links, include design and engineering, production, accounting and finance, and marketing. Some of the main areas of interaction are summarised in Table 1.1.

Table 1.1 *Purchasing's links with internal customers*

INTERNAL CUSTOMER	LINKS WITH PURCHASING
Design and engineering	• Value engineering and value analysis • Quality assurance • Evaluation of availability and price of materials • Preparation of specifications
Production	• Preparation of delivery schedules • Control of inventory and scrap • Make or buy decisions • Cooperation in implementing world class manufacturing techniques • Planning to avoid costly special production runs
Accounting and finance	• Budget preparation, and monitoring of actual input costs against budget • Administration of buying, eg in processing of invoices and progress payments • Stock valuation, stocktaking and insurance of stock
Marketing	• Purchasing's role in enhancing product features, particularly price • Ensuring prompt deliveries in to meet promised deadlines for delivery out • Cooperation on reciprocal trading

1.27 Poor relationships between purchasing and other departments will lead to inadequate understanding by purchasing of requirements elsewhere in the organisation and inefficiency in translating these requirements into the necessary materials support actions.

1.28 The other side of the coin is that purchasing's own activities will be hampered through inadequate information, and in extreme cases by actual obstruction caused by inter-departmental frictions.

1.29 A traditional example is the conflict that sometimes arises between production and sales departments. To secure a particular sale, it may be necessary to institute a special production run. This may be resisted by production staff wishing to optimise the efficient running of their own department, with insufficient regard to overall corporate profitability.

Information networks

1.30 A great aid to reducing conflict and increasing communication and cooperation with internal customers is provided by information networks – in which different managers and different departments can all hook on to the same central information source. A network is merely a means of connecting together two or more computers.

1.31 In detail, the following operational benefits may be expected from such systems when dealing with internal customers.

- Reduction in the time spent by purchasing staff on clerical tasks such as order processing and expediting
- Increased time available to purchasing staff for value added activities where their professional expertise can enhance organisational performance
- Dramatic reduction in delivery times to, say, production departments by increased speed of processing orders
- Dramatic reduction in costs and other problems associated with high volumes of paperwork.

Managing the service provided by purchasing

1.32 If purchasing is regarded as providing a service to internal customers, then it is appropriate to manage the service, just as if we were servicing an external client. One important step to this end would be a system of measurement and control.

1.33 There are various measures that could be used to evaluate the effectiveness of purchasing's service to its internal customers. Here are some possibilities.

- Average lapse of time between requisition and delivery
- Average cost of processing a requisition through to delivery
- Number of complaints from user departments
- Cost savings achieved for user departments

1.34 The task of managing the purchasing function naturally falls to the Head of Purchasing, whose task includes ensuring a quality service for internal users of the purchasing service. As part of this process, Head of Purchasing has a duty to communicate effectively with users of the purchasing service.

2 Devolved purchasers

What is meant by devolved purchasing?

2.1 In some organisations, all purchasing activities are routed through a single specialised purchasing department. This is called **centralisation** of the purchasing function. In others, many different user departments become involved in purchasing activities. This is called **decentralisation** of the purchasing function.

2.2 In practice there is a spectrum of possibilities between full centralisation and full decentralisation. Unless an organisation is at the extreme 'centralisation' end of the spectrum, devolved purchasing will be present. The term refers to purchasing activities undertaken by people who are not members of the purchasing function, and whose main activities are nothing to do with purchasing. (You may also come across the term **part-time purchasing** to describe this.)

2.3 Why does devolved purchasing take place? There are three main reasons.

- In some organisations, devolved purchasing was a regular occurrence at a time before the introduction of a dedicated purchasing function. (Remember that the development of the purchasing profession is a relatively recent trend.) In such organisations, a legacy of devolved purchasing remains for historical reasons.
- Sometimes it is found that user departments believe themselves best qualified to make purchasing decisions. This is particularly the case where the items to be purchased are very technical in nature: users may not trust the purchasing function to have sufficient technical understanding.
- Finally, there is the phenomenon of 'maverick spending': users sometimes deliberately keep spending decisions away from the purchasing department. This may be because they simply wish to keep power in their own hands, or may reflect distrust of purchasing's objectives, which are sometimes perceived to be solely concerned with cost reduction.

Advantages and disadvantages of devolved purchasing

2.4 There are obvious disadvantages associated with devolved purchasing.

- There is a high risk of committing company funds unwisely if the people responsible for spending have no professional expertise.
- There is a risk that a part-time purchaser is too preoccupied with his main role to give sufficient attention to his purchasing activities.
- There are serious difficulties in budgeting and controlling spend if responsibilities for purchasing are dispersed throughout the organisation.

2.5 However, it would be foolish to disregard the existence of devolved purchasing, and given that it exists, it makes sense to identify any advantages that it may bring.

- In the case of routine, low-value purchases it may be sensible to devolve responsibility to user departments. This frees up time for professional purchasers to devote to more difficult tasks.
- It is no bad thing to take advantage of the technical skills and knowledge that may be spread throughout the organisation. Devolved purchasing, if properly controlled, is a way of achieving this.
- The purchasing function should be concerned to communicate purchasing disciplines as far as possible throughout the organisation. Once again, a properly controlled devolved purchasing operation may be a means to this end.

3 The decision making unit (DMU)

Introduction

3.1 Organisational or business-to-business buying behaviour (ie one organisation buying from another organisation) displays many complexities which we will now go on to discuss. In your role as a purchaser you may be aware of the factors we are about to discuss.

3.2 Organisational buying is different from consumer buying because purchases are not made for personal consumption, but instead for:

- incorporation into other products – materials or components
- organisational consumption – office supplies, consulting services
- use – installations or equipment
- resale.

3.3 While you are reading this section, you should also bear in mind certain other characteristics of business-to-business markets.

- Buyers are few in number, but may be large in scale.
- Derived demand is in force – the ultimate consumer demands Product X, so the organisational buyer demands Component Y in order to manufacture X. The demand for Y is derived from the demand for X.
- Demand may be inelastic, in that an organisation may be unable to continue in operation unless it is able to purchase the goods and services it requires.
- Industrial and organisational purchasers are usually more knowledgeable than consumers about their products and sources of supply.

3.4 The role of personal selling is significant in business-to-business buying. With regard to promotional activities, the emphasis usually switches from mass advertising (as in consumer markets) to an emphasis on the salesforce. The marketer can also benefit from the knowledge and information gained by the salesforce through personal communication with the buying organisation. This is sometimes not recognised by organisations and a valuable source of information to help with future marketing planning is under-utilised.

Multiple buying influences

3.5 Influences on organisational buying are often divided into four categories. These categories are displayed in Figure 1.1 and we shall discuss each of the areas in turn.

Figure 1.1 *Multiple influences on organisational buying behaviour*

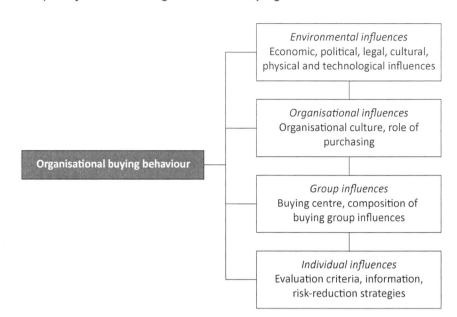

Environmental buying influences

3.6 There are six major environmental influences and these are indicated in Figure 1.1. In relation to economic factors, the condition of the economy is characterised by various elements such as employment, prices, income levels etc. We need to think about how the economic climate influences organisational buyer behaviour.

3.7 Organisational demand is derived from the demand for consumer goods and so, as in consumer markets, the state of the economy influences an organisation's willingness to purchase. For example, in a recession organisations may not want to invest in plant and equipment.

3.8 Economic influences become more complicated when the organisation is buying internationally. It is then at the mercy of currency fluctuations which may not only delay the purchase, but may encourage the organisation to start sourcing domestically.

3.9 The **political and legal environment**, which includes government spending, taxation and import and export controls, should be evaluated for its influence upon buying decisions. An example familiar to purchasing professionals is the impact of compulsory competitive tendering on the organisational buying process.

3.10 **Culture** influences the way organisations purchase because the buyers in the organisation are individuals who have learned and acquired cultural norms and values. Culture affects the way these individuals react to the environment.

3.11 **Physical influences** include such elements as climate and the geographical location of the organisation. Buyer behaviour can be influenced by the fact that the organisation utilises suppliers that are geographically close. This may be important for the purpose of building relationships or if the organisation operates a just in time system which benefits from geographical closeness.

3.12 **Technological influences** can cause many changes to organisational buyer behaviour. Developments in technology can change the methods the buyer uses to purchase, the people involved in the purchase process and their relative importance. Marketers monitor these changes and adjust their marketing efforts accordingly.

Organisational influences

3.13 An **organisation's culture** will evolve from its objectives, procedures, organisation structures and internal systems. Marketers should be familiar with these aspects if they seek to satisfy the organisation's needs. This will be particularly appropriate in the case of personal selling so that the sales representative of the marketing organisation can tailor a selling strategy to fit the culture of each organisation he is selling to. For instance, some organisations encourage innovation and allow employees to operate their own systems while others have strict procedures that must be followed.

3.14 The **role of purchasing** in organisations will vary. Think about your role as a purchaser and where you fit in the organisation. Purchasing is sometimes seen as an essential strategic area while in other organisations it might occupy a low position in the management hierarchy. In some organisations purchasing is centralised while in others it is decentralised.

3.15 In general terms, the centralised purchasing function will be specialised. This means that strategic purchasing specialists have a knowledge of supply and demand conditions, vendors, supplier cost factors and other information relevant to the supplier environments. To the marketer, who is the supplier, this will have a strong influence on the way he markets and sells to the organisation.

3.16 If purchasing is centralised, the industrial marketer may have fewer buyers to deal with and may be able to identify these buyers' objectives. Therefore, the marketer's selling strategy should parallel the buying organisation's purchasing function. National account management programmes may be adopted so that effective relationships can be developed.

Group influences

3.17 Organisational buyers are strongly influenced by group members. These groups are formed of anyone who participates in making organisational purchase decisions. Again, this has ramifications for the sales person in that he must establish what organisational members take part in the buying process and what their influence is in the buying decision (composition of group).

3.18 The **buying centre/DMU** usually includes several participants who will have different interests, authority and persuasiveness and these participants will be different in each buying situation. The size of the buying centre varies and will be related to the type of purchase that is being undertaken. Three types commonly identified, in increasing order of complexity, are as follows.

- **Straight rebuy** – this involves a routine purchase of something that has been bought before and that involves no risk.
- **Modified rebuy** – this involves the purchase of something the same as has been bought before but from a different supplier (say because the original supplier failed to meet quality standards), or slightly different to what was bought before but from the same supplier (say because the user's needs have changed).
- **New buy** – this involves the purchase of something for which previously there had been no need. It may or may not have great financial and strategic impact. A great deal of work will go into all stages of the buying process, in particular the information search and specification stages.

3.19 These factors make the marketer's job complex because each individual is important at different stages during the purchasing process. As an example, a design engineer may be more influential at the early stages in the process when product specifications are being drawn up but may be less influential during negotiations. The marketer or his sales representative will have to understand the buying situation and the information that is required by the organisation if he is to anticipate the size and composition of the buying centre. This becomes even more complex if the buying centre evolves during the purchasing process rather than at the beginning, and if the buying centre varies from one organisation to another as well as from one purchasing situation to another.

3.20 The **composition of the DMU** may be difficult to determine and so the industrial sales person may communicate directly with the organisational buyer firstly before communicating with other members of the buying group. He must then establish the roles played by each member of the buying group.

3.21 The sales person must remember that each member of the buying centre may evaluate products using different criteria and that the motivations of group members are the same as for individual consumers because each group member is an individual. Whatever information the sales person can discover about personalities and group dynamics will be useful in trying to influence their buying behaviour.

Individual influences

3.22 It is the individuals in an organisation that make buying decisions, not the organisation itself. Each individual will have their own function, personality and perception of how best to achieve purchasing objectives in a particular buying situation. The marketer must attempt to understand the individual perceptions of each group member in the buying situation.

3.23 **Evaluation criteria** are the specifications that are used to compare industrial products and services. They will differ for each individual. The sales person may have to learn each person's criteria and also how to be effective with each person. This is a difficult task and may require an understanding of the motivations of each individual so that the sales person can communicate effectively with each group member and prepare an effective marketing strategy.

3.24 Hutt and Speh (in *Business Marketing Management*) discuss the different types of motivation for individuals.

Rational motives

- Price
- Quality
- Service
- Continuity of supply
- Reciprocity

Emotional motives

- Status and rewards
- Perceived risk
- Friendship

3.25 The marketing organisation may find that the sales person's knowledge of evaluation criteria of buying centre members can be used when designing new products and when developing and targeting advertising and future personal selling presentations.

3.26 The **information** that the marketer supplies to a buying organisation includes mailshots, advertising, and personal sales presentations. However, each individual in the buying centre will not pay attention to, understand or retain all of this information.

3.27 Often, a buying situation takes place over a period of time (for example in the purchase of a major piece of industrial equipment). Marketing communications must be carefully designed and targeted. This is a complex process because each individual will have his own information needs and the marketer must ascertain these needs and attempt to understand when the need will occur. In addition, no two buying centres will be the same and the length of the buying process will differ from organisation to organisation.

3.28 Individuals are often motivated by a desire to reduce the **level of risk** in purchasing decisions. They might visit the marketer's plant, talk to other buyers and use multiple sources in order to reduce the level of risk involved in making a wrong decision.

3.29 Because of these factors, the organisational buyers may rely on familiar suppliers. The marketer must do everything possible to keep this loyalty and maintain the relationship. Again, the sales person may have to play a significant role in this area.

3.30 The marketer should also consider the level of risk that their product may evoke in each buying situation so that when new products are being designed or new customers are being approached the marketer can evaluate the impact of alternative strategies on perceived risk.

The organisational DMU

3.31 The DMU or buying centre includes any individual who participates in the buying decision and these individuals will fulfil one or more of the following buying roles.

- **Users**: individuals who will use the product or service
- **Influencers**: individuals who provide technical expertise and influence the buying decision
- **Deciders**: individuals who decide on product requirements and suppliers
- **Buyers:** individuals who actually place the order and take part in negotiations
- **Gatekeepers**: individuals who distribute or inhibit the flow of information to members of the DMU.

3.32 The DMU will vary according to different purchase situations and we have already discussed the multiple buying influences on each member of the DMU and the resulting complexities for the marketer.

The organisational buying process

3.33 This process is depicted in Figure 1.2. The major differences (compared with consumer buying) include the fact that this process is normally more formal in an organisation, more participants are involved and it takes longer to complete.

Figure 1.2 *Organisational buying process*

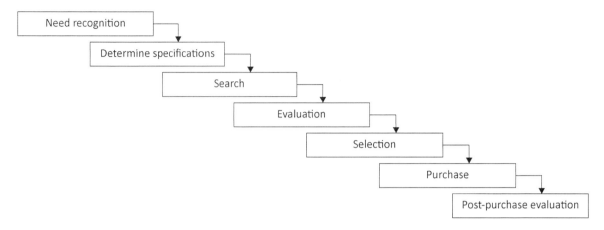

3.34 Need recognition occurs when an organisation identifies a need that can be satisfied by the purchase of a product or service. Often needs are identified by the eventual users of the product or service being purchased. Specifications will then be established so that the exact requirements of the organisation are detailed. This may take place with the aid of a sales person from a supplier organisation.

3.35 In the search stage buyers will use many sources of information or may request tenders. Evaluation should be systematic and may use some form of supplier evaluation technique. At this stage there may be negotiation about the price and/or the original specifications. Once selection has taken place and the product delivered, the organisation will evaluate the product. The marketer will want the post-purchase evaluation to be positive to ensure a loyal buying organisation and in order to maintain the relationship.

3.36 This is a general overview of the purchasing process. The number of people involved (the DMU) and the time taken to complete the process will depend very much on the type of product and the importance of that product to the organisation. The marketer must monitor the process so that he can offer information, and negotiate and communicate at the right times and with the right information.

4 Account management

How many 'touch points'?

4.1 There are various ways of allocating and structuring contact between a buying organisation and its suppliers. We will look at some of the options, focusing on the one specified by the syllabus: the role of account manager.

4.2 One of the first questions to ask is how many contacts or 'touch points' there should be between the buying and supplying organisation. When the buyer wants to get in touch with a supplier, does he have one contact to deal with (say, an account manager) – or a directory of different contacts for different purposes? Are other people in the buying organisation (eg user departments, the accounts department, goods inwards) also in contact with the supplier at relevant points – or are all contacts channelled through the buyer, vendor manager or contract manager (the buyer-side equivalent of an account manager)?

4.3 In general, it is good to co-ordinate or centralise contacts. A **single point of contact** (SPOC) approach means that a supplier uses the purchasing function as the only communications interface with the customer: the buyer is the 'gatekeeper' controlling all dealings with the supplier organisation. This has certain benefits, especially for relatively small, centralised operations.

- People know who their contact is.
- There is added value in a 'one stop shop' level of service, rather than being handed from department to department.
- There is less likelihood of inconsistent or conflicting requirements or information being communicated by different contacts.
- There is greater ownership and accountability for supplier management.
- Repeated contact with the same person enables familiarity and trust to be built up over time, as the foundation for a deepening relationship.

4.4 However, contacts may perform a range of different roles in relationship management: enquiry; order or payment chasing; problem-solving; complaint and adjustment; feedback-seeking and feedback-giving; information exchange; negotiation; networking and influence-seeking; interpersonal relationship and trust development (eg via social and 'touching-base' contacts); and so on. Some of these contacts will involve different functions and sites, and it may be inefficient to route all communication, for all purposes, through a single point of contact. As the complexity of markets, organisations and products and services increases, a SPOC approach becomes increasingly difficult. The alternative of *decentralised* contact, via multiple contacts or touch points, allows:

- Diverse inputs to supplier relationships for different purposes and at different levels of expertise (so that a supplier can talk to a commodity specialist, engineer, quality manager or accounts person when necessary)
- Avoidance of communication 'bottlenecks' where a single contact is overburdened
- Better relationship and knowledge continuity, if a single contact leaves or is unavailable.

4.5 In order to get the best of both worlds, and minimise the drawbacks of each, the best approach may be **co-ordinated decentralisation**. In other words, you set up multiple contact points and communication channels – but you ensure that coherent and consistent messages are being given across them all, by setting up efficient cross-functional information-sharing and relationship management systems: cross-functional purchasing teams, cross-organisational new product development teams and project steering committees, and database information management systems.

The account manager

4.6 One way of structuring contact in long-term relationships is to use 'account managers', individuals (either on the buyer or the supplier side, or both) who are responsible for managing and co-ordinating the overall relationship on behalf of their organisation. Account management had its roots in customer relations, where the marketing organisation nominated individuals to manage relationships with key account customers: you might be familiar with this in banks and advertising agencies, for example. The concept is now being applied to supplier relations as well.

4.7 The role of account manager (who may be called a vendor manager, on the buyer side) will typically include the following tasks.

- Managing all aspects of the relationship between the supplier and the buyer, and between the supplier and the buyer's internal customers: acting as liaison between them

- Managing project and relationship processes (contact structures; cross-functional teamworking; communication channels; collaborative planning, decision-making and conflict resolution mechanisms and so on)
- Acting as a single point of contact and information for all internal and external stakeholders in the relationship
- Acting as a champion of the relationship to senior management (eg recommending the supplier for projects, reporting on the relationship to senior management or securing executive sponsorship of a partnership)
- Ensuring delivery of goods and services according to agreed terms and standards (perhaps liaising with a contract manager)
- Managing the development of the relationship through maintaining rapport, developing trust, and proactively managing tensions and conflicts
- Encouraging the supplier to adhere to agreed standards or KPIs, and to seek ongoing improvements in performance through the duration of the relationship (eg initiating and gaining supplier buy-in to cost reduction, continuous improvement or innovation programmes)
- Monitoring, reviewing and drawing learning from the relationship.

4.8 An account manager therefore requires a range of skills and attributes such as: knowledge of the products or services purchased; knowledge of the customer or supplier and its transaction history; an understanding of contracts; project management skills; and good interpersonal and networking skills.

4.9 The benefits of customer or supplier account management include the following.

- Better control over the performance of contracts, and changes to plans and specifications
- Maintaining communication during the supply relationship, with potential to develop goodwill, trust and deepening collaboration over time
- Greater responsiveness and speed of problem-solving, with a single 'hub' for contact with the organisation who is familiar with the account and its potential issues
- Added value through planned improvements and well-managed relationships and work flows
- The ability to anticipate performance and relationship problems early, and to deal with them before they become serious.

4.10 Account management represents an extra level of investment, and will therefore not be necessary or viable for all supply chain relationships. It is generally applied only to key account customers (high value, high frequency, high status) and strategic or critical suppliers.

Chapter summary

- Purchasing has a number of internal customers: functions and departments for which it provides services, such as buying materials.
- Typical customers of purchasing are: design and engineering; production; accounting and finance; and marketing.
- Devolved purchasing carries risks because there is no professional purchasing involvement. Despite this, there are some advantages in devolved purchasing provided that it is properly controlled.
- Organisational buying is very different from consumer buying. In particular, the decision making unit within an organisation will typically comprise a number of individuals rather than a single person.
- Influences on organisational buying behaviour are sometimes categorised as environmental influences, organisation influences, group influences and individual influences.
- The relationship between a buyer and a supplier must be managed systematically. Account management brings many benefits to both parties.

Self-test questions

Numbers in brackets refer to paragraphs where you can check your answers.

1   Give an example of an internal supplier and internal customer. (1.7)

2   List the primary roles of a purchasing function. (1.17)

3   List typical internal customers of purchasing. (1.26)

4   Give reasons why devolved purchasing takes place. (2.3)

5   List (a) advantages and (b) disadvantages of devolved purchasing. (2.4, 2.5)

6   Give four categories of influence on organisational buying behaviour. (3.5)

7   List the five roles in the organisational DMU. (3.31)

8   What are the benefits of a SPOC approach to account management? (4.3)

9   List tasks typically undertaken by an account manager. (4.7)

10 List benefits of account management. (4.9)

CHAPTER 2

Stakeholders

Assessment criteria and indicative content

 Classify the stakeholders in a relationship between purchasers and suppliers

- Defining stakeholders
- Classifying internal and external stakeholders
- The RACI (responsible, accountable, consulted, informed) model as a classification tool
- Communicating with stakeholders

Section headings

1   Defining stakeholders
2   Classifying stakeholders
3   The RACI model
4   Communicating with stakeholders

1   Defining stakeholders

Key stakeholder groups

1.1   Stakeholders are individuals or groups who have a legitimate interest or 'stake' in an organisation, project or decision. They may have invested money in it, or contributed to it, or they may be affected by its activities and outcomes.

1.2   The stakeholders of an organisation include internal, connected and external groups.

- **Internal stakeholders** are members of the organisation: the directors, managers and employees who operate within the organisation's boundaries. Key internal stakeholders in purchasing plans and activities include: senior management (who need purchasing to do its job in order for overall corporate strategies to be fulfilled); purchasing managers (who are responsible for purchasing performance); and the managers and staff of other functions or units of the organisation whose work and goals intersect with those of the purchasing function.
- **Connected stakeholders** have direct legal, contractual or commercial dealings with the organisation. They include: shareholders (the owners of the firm) and other financiers, such as banks; customers and consumers; suppliers; and distributors.
- **External or secondary stakeholders** do not have direct contractual or commercial dealings with the organisation, but have an interest in, or are affected by, its activities. They include: the government and regulatory bodies (which seek to control business activity); professional bodies and trade unions (which represent the interests of their members within the organisation); various interest and pressure groups (which promote and protect the interests of their members, or a particular cause); and the local community (within which the organisation operates).

1.3 If asked in the exam about external stakeholders who impact on, or are impacted by, purchasing activity, don't neglect the secondary stakeholders. The widening of an organisation's responsibilities to these less directly connected groups is a major trend in modern business, under the name of 'corporate social responsibility' (CSR) – and CIPS takes it very seriously.

1.4 Stakeholders are *affected by* the organisation's activities in different ways and to different degrees. Any given stakeholder group will have a bundle of needs, wants, expectations and concerns in regard to the organisation: 'interests' which the group will seek to protect or promote in their relationship with the organisation. So, for example, suppliers will have an interest in efficient information flows, payment as agreed, fair treatment of tenders, and mutually beneficial ongoing business. Customers will have an interest in safe and satisfying products and services, value for money, ethical business dealings and so on.

1.5 Stakeholders also have power to *affect* the organisation's activities in different ways and to different degrees. Financiers have the power to withhold resources if their needs are not met. Customers can similarly withhold their custom and support. Suppliers influence the quality, cost and timely availability of products and services, and therefore the organisation's competitive advantage. And so on.

1.6 Let's briefly survey the interests and influence of some of the main stakeholders in purchasing activities and performance.

Internal stakeholders

1.7 Internal stakeholders include general groups such as managers and employees (and/or volunteer workers or other types of members, in not-for-profit organisations). For example, the procurement function may have to market itself to senior management or management teams, or may have to communicate changes in purchasing policy and procedures to all staff.

1.8 More specifically, the internal supply chain and cross-functional activity in the organisation means that other functional departments are key internal stakeholders in procurement activity and performance.

1.9 The interests and influence of these various internal stakeholder groups are summarised in Table 2.1.

Table 2.1 *Internal stakeholders*

STAKEHOLDER	INTERESTS/NEEDS/DRIVERS	INFLUENCE/CONTRIBUTION
Directors/ managers	• The organisation's profitability, survival and growt • Fulfilment of objectives and projects for which they are responsible (requiring purchasing inputs and/or support)	• Formal authority over planning • Shape the commitment and motivation of staff • Influence through politics, networking and influencing skills
Staff/team members or other organisation members	• The organisation's profitability and survival, for continued employment • Support, information and inputs to fulfil task goals and earn rewards • Healthy and safe working environment • Fair and ethical treatment	• Scarce resource: competitive edge in times or areas of skill shortage • Threat of withdrawn labour • Potential to add value through skilled, motivated performance, flexibility etc (especially in services)
Technical/design function	• Accurate fulfilment of specifications • Timely, relevant, expert advice on price and availability issues • Connection to suppliers who might contribute innovation and expertise	• Determine specifications and materials which the buyer will have to translate into purchase orders
Manufacture/ production/ operations function	• Right inputs at right price and right quality, delivered to right place at right time to maintain efficient flow of production • Supplier management and SCM to support flexibility, JIT supply, innovation etc. • Sourcing and procurement services (eg for capital equipment) or consultancy	• Key internal customer: purchasing performance measured by fulfilment of 'five rights' • Provision of feedback on quality of inputs to aid supplier and contract management
Sales and marketing function	• Quality, customisation and delivery levels that will satisfy customers • Fulfilment of promises made to customers; responsiveness to feedback and demands • Information on products and delivery schedules for promotions • Sourcing and procurement services (eg printing services, office supplies, sales force cars) or consultancy (eg for own media space buying or agency selection)	• Provision of market research and customer feedback information to influence product specifications and quality management • Promises made to customers via marketing communications, which purchasing must contribute to delivering
Finance/admin function	• Adherence to financial procedures (eg budgetary control, invoicing arrangements) • Notification of terms negotiated with suppliers (eg discounts, payment terms) • Support for cost control and/or reduction • Provision of info for budgetary control, costing, credit control etc • Sourcing and procurement services (eg for IT systems and stationery) or consultancy	• Control or influence budget allocations • Action payment of suppliers • May impact on supplier relationships (eg if payment for supplies is late or withheld) • May be leaders or champions of cost control and reduction initiatives
Storage and distribution (or logistics) – if not part of purchasing and supply function	• Timely info about incoming and outgoing orders, for transport and storage planning • Policies for 'green' transport planning, safe goods handling etc. • Sourcing and procurement services (eg for equipment) or consultancy	• Control or influence timely flow of incoming and outgoing deliveries • Influence on wastage, damage and obsolescence of supplies (eg through safe, secure, efficient transport and storage)

Connected stakeholders

1.10 Connected stakeholders often have a significant stake in organisational activity, by virtue of their contractual or commercial relationships with the organisation. Some of the interests and influence of these groups are summarised in Table 2.2.

Table 2.2 *Connected stakeholders*

STAKEHOLDER	INTERESTS/NEEDS/DRIVERS	INFLUENCE/CONTRIBUTION
Shareholders	• Return on investment, dividends • Corporate governance: transparency, accountability, directors protecting their interests	• Owners and financiers of firms • Voting power at company meetings • Power to sell shares (influencing share price, perceptions of financial markets)
End customers	• Satisfaction of a complex bundle of expectations and motives for purchase (eg value for money, quality, service experience) – NB different for consumer and business or industrial buyers.	• Focus of all business activity • Source of sales revenue and profits • Source of feedback information (via surveys, complaints etc) • Power to switch or withdraw custom
Intermediary customers (eg agents, distributors, retail outlets)	• Ethical, efficient trading practices and systems • Sales support: product info, reliable supply, promotional support, sales force training • Earnings and profits (eg through discount margins, fees or commissions) • Mutually beneficial ongoing relationship	• Help to promote and distribute products • Part of total customer 'value delivery system' for competitive advantage • Potential for collaborative promotion • Source of feedback info on sales, customers etc • Power to withhold distribution or promotion, or to aid competitors (eg with exclusive distribution deals)
Suppliers	• Clear specifications (fewer disputes) • Efficient transaction and relationship handling • Fair procedures for awarding contracts • Timely payment of debts • Opportunities for reasonable profit taking • Opportunities for development through regular trading, alliance or partnership • Feedback info to support service	• Provision of potentially key inputs (at required quality, price, time) • Power to withhold or restrict supply • Expertise (eg for product development and specification) • Potential for added value (eg via JIT, lean supply, collaborative waste reduction, continuous improvement)
Financial institutions/ lenders	• Financial strength and stability of the company (for security of the loan) • Return on investment (eg via interest) • Mutually beneficial ongoing relationship	• Short-term and long-term loan finance to maintain and develop operations • Added value services (eg insurance, currency management) • Power to restrict or withdraw credit facilities

External stakeholders

1.11 As we mentioned earlier, the view of what constitutes a legitimate stakeholder has broadened from a focus on groups involved directly with the organisation, function or project to a wider range of groups who are less directly affected by its activities and their results. You may be able to think of examples where public, consumer or interest group pressure has resulted in a change of corporate policy: opposition to genetically modified foods; boycotts of Shell (over incidents of environmental damage) and Nike (over allegations of worker exploitation); and so on.

1.12 Businesses have, in particular, become increasingly aware of the need to maintain a positive reputation in the marketplace, and this may require a more inclusive approach to stakeholder management, which recognises the legitimate needs and concerns of wider, secondary or 'indirect' stakeholders.

1.13 External stakeholders are likely to have quite diverse objectives and degrees of influence. Some of these are summarised in Table 2.3.

Table 2.3 *External stakeholders*

STAKEHOLDER	INTERESTS/NEEDS/DRIVERS	INFLUENCE/CONTRIBUTION
Government and regulatory bodies	• Corporate tax revenue • Healthy level of economic activity • Compliance with legislation and regulation • Reports and returns • Support for community development and employment	• Power to enforce requirements through legislation, regulation, penalties • Control over tax levels and public funding (eg via grants) • Bargaining power as a large customer or supplier of goods or services • Support and guidance for business
Pressure groups (eg Greenpeace) and interest groups (eg consumer associations, trade unions)	• Promotion and increased awareness of a cause or issue (eg fair trade, environment) • Protection of rights and interests of members • Access to information and accountability • Sponsorship or donation funding	• May shape policy (eg via lobbying) • Inform and mobilise public and consumer opinion for or against the organisation • Source of info re issues and impacts • May collaborate to enhance ethical credentials of the firm or brand • Power to mobilise protests or boycotts
Community and society at large	• Access to products and services, employment • Product safety • Affordability of essential goods and services • Socially responsible business and environmental practices: harm minimisation	• Pool of current and potential customers, suppliers and employees • Power to mobilise government policy and consumer opinion

2 Classifying stakeholders

2.1 From our discussion of stakeholder interests and influence above, it is clear that it is important for the legitimate interests and expectations of stakeholder groups to be taken into account, for ethical and commercial reasons.

2.2 However, the interests and expectations of stakeholder groups will often be different – and even conflicting. Shareholders, for example, will want to maximise profits (to increase the value of their shares), while suppliers will want to protect their own profit margins; interest groups may resist profit-taking at the expense of the environment; and employees may want to maximise their pay and conditions. Similarly, in the case of procurement stakeholders, the marketing function may want to maximise customisation and delivery-on-demand, while the operations function wants to be able to plan ahead and reduce variances, while the finance function wants to cut costs. You can't please all of the stakeholders all of the time.

2.3 Boddy (*Management: An Introduction*) concludes: 'The overall message is that it is important to the long-run success of organisations to embrace stakeholder expectations, but that the degree of priority they give to each is unequal and changing (over time).' The most common method of prioritising stakeholder relationships is stakeholder classification or mapping.

The power/interest matrix

2.4 Mendelow's power/interest matrix is a useful tool for classifying stakeholders according to:

- Their power to influence organisational (or purchasing) activity and
- The likelihood that they will use that power: that is, the strength of their interest in a given issue or decision.

2.5 You simply draw up a blank two-by-two matrix and, for any given situation, allocate each relevant stakeholder group to the quadrant which best describes their power/interest level. Each quadrant comes with a recommended relationship management strategy, which we have inserted into the matrix: Figure 2.1.

Figure 2.1 *Mendelow's power/interest matrix*

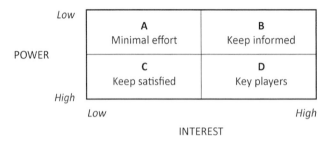

2.6 Working through each of the segments in turn.

- Stakeholders with neither power nor interest (A) are a low-priority group: resources will not be wasted taking their goals or potential response into account. Small investors, or large suppliers with whom the organisation only does a small volume of business, may be in this category. So too may the local community or other organisational functions, in relation to particular decisions with low immediate impacts on them.
- Stakeholders in Segment B are important because of their high interest: they may have low direct influence, but unless they are kept 'in the loop' and understand the need for decisions, they may seek additional power by lobbying or banding together to protect their interest. Community, small supplier and employee groups may be in this category, in relation to decisions which impact significantly on their interests. The recommended strategy is to keep them informed of plans and outcomes, through stakeholder marketing, communication and education programmes (discussed later in the chapter).
- Stakeholders in Segment C are important because of their high influence: they currently have low interest, but if dissatisfied or concerned, their interest may be aroused. A large institutional shareholder, or large supplier, may be in this category, as may government agencies and regulatory bodies (if the organisation is broadly compliant). Senior managers in departments not directly affected by a procurement decision may also fall into this category. The recommended strategy is to keep these stakeholders satisfied, so that they do not need to exert their influence.
- Stakeholders in Segment D are known as 'key players': they have influence and are motivated to use it in their own interests. Major customers, key suppliers and intermediaries, senior procurement managers and strategic allies or partners may be in this category. The recommended strategy is one of early involvement and participation, so that the stakeholder's goals can be integrated with organisational goals as far as possible – securing support, rather than resistance.

Stakeholder position analysis

2.7 Another tool for classifying stakeholders is Egan's 'stakeholders in change' model. Stakeholders are divided into nine distinct groups, in relation to a leader or agent of change.

- Partners support the change agent.
- Allies will support the change agent, given encouragement.
- Fellow travellers are passive supporters, who may be committed to the change, but not to the change agent in particular.
- Bedfellows support the change, but do not know or trust the change agent.
- Fence sitters are those whose allegiances are not yet clear.
- Loose cannons may vote either way on changes in which they have no direct stake.
- Opponents oppose the change, but not the change agent in particular.
- Adversaries oppose the change agent and the change.
- The Voiceless are 'silent' stakeholders who are affected by the change, but lack advocates or power to influence decisions. (Examples may include children affected by toxic materials used in toy manufacture, or wildlife affected by the disposal of waste products.)

2.8 Like Mendelow, Egan argues that different groups should be managed differently.

- Supporters (in various groups) must be encouraged and kept 'on side'. Partners may not require much interaction, but the organisation cannot afford to lose their interest or support. Allies require some encouragement, but infrequent contact (a 'light touch') is usually sufficient. Passive supporters (fellow travellers and bedfellows) require more intensive rapport- and relationship-building contacts to mobilise their commitment.
- Fence sitters may or may not have the potential to become valuable supporters or harmful opponents. The potential value of their allegiance, or potential cost of their resistance, will determine how much is invested in communication.
- Opponents need to be 'converted' by persuading them of the merits of the change and addressing their reasons for resistance. This is often done via formal, structured communication (eg meetings for negotiation and conflict resolution). Adversaries, on the other hand, may be too difficult and costly to 'win over', and may have to be marginalised or otherwise neutralised, so they cannot mobilise further opposition.
- The view of corporate ethics and social responsibility is that the needs of the voiceless should also receive attention, despite their relative powerlessness. Again, low-frequency contact should be all that is necessary to monitor the response of these stakeholders or their advocates and allow them to feel heard.

3   The RACI model

Defining RACI

3.1 The RACI (pronounced 'racey') model/matrix, also known as a Responsibility Assignment Matrix, describes the various roles in completing tasks or deliverables for a business process or project. From the title Responsibility Assignment Matrix it is clear that the matrix is about assigning responsibility within a particular project. RACI is a way of categorising stakeholders to help define their roles and responsibilities.

3.2 The RACI matrix can be used in a wide variety of business functions and is especially useful in clarifying roles and responsibilities in cross-functional or departmental projects and processes. In general terms the purpose is to manage project stakeholders and their expectations and to ensure clear and accurate project information is given out.

The RACI chart

3.3 In understanding current processes, as well as in designing new processes, it is important to recognise the roles and responsibilities required. To this end, processes can be flowcharted and then mapped using a RACI chart in order to understand and clarify responsibilities.

3.4 The RACI chart allows for each task step to be identified; then each stakeholder and their responsibilities can be identified. The resulting chart can be scrutinised for opportunities for improvement.

3.5 With a standard RACI, there are four responsibilities and issues to consider with each opportunity.

3.6 **Responsible (R).** This is the person or group responsible for performing a task. This area is to define who is responsible for ensuring the successful completion of a task. There are situations in business where responsibilities are shared or vague, the result being confusion, conflict or a poor outcome. If there are too many people with responsibility with little or no coordination and oversight to ensure that the task is completed then the result will be as before. What is required is clarity of responsibility and this approach underpins RACI.

3.7 **Accountable (A).** This is the person who is held accountable for the task being complete. In some cases, risks can be managed by segregating the responsible and accountable roles. In general, one person should be accountable for a task being performed. At the same time, if a person is accountable for most of the steps in a procedure, one must consider if there is a segregation of duties issue wherein the person(s) controls too much.

3.8 **Consulted (C).** These are the people communicated with prior to a task being performed. Essentially, their input is sought and factored in prior to any action. As the number of parties consulted increases, the speed with which action can be taken decreases. Conversely, if too few people are consulted, improper decisions may be made. Typically management are accountable and they will want a clear, concise summary of progress and what risks there might be to a successful project conclusion.

3.9 **Informed (I).** These are the parties who are notified about a task after it has been performed. This is usually the largest group and as stakeholders they require effective communication and management. If the correct parties are not informed in some situations, then incidents can arise from groups wondering what has changed. At the same time, if there are lots of people being informed, is it necessary? Usually the end users of the project and their support and commitment must be built over time starting from awareness, through understanding to mobilisation for change.

3.10 **Supports (S).** Some groups add this in as a fifth responsibility. It refers to a person or group who provide resources for a task to be completed. When charts include this category, they are referred to as 'RASCI charts', but otherwise are identical to RACI charts.

RACI in action

3.11 A RACI analysis is useful in the following situations.

- Workload analysis: when used against individuals or departments overloads can be quickly identified.
- Re-organisation: to ensure that key functions and processes are not overlooked.

- Employee turnover: newcomers can quickly identify their roles and responsibilities.
- Work assignment: allows duties to be redistributed effectively between groups and individuals.
- Project management: allows for flexibility in matrix management situations, allowing for the right balance between line and project accountabilities.
- Conflict resolution: provides a forum for discussion and resolving inter-departmental conflict.
- Documenting the *status quo*: the output from RACI is a simple yet effective method of documenting the roles and responsibilities in an organisation.

3.12 A RACI exercise is carried out by identifying the functions and processes within the organisation or department and describing the key activities taking place. Each activity or decision is described using a suitable action verb such as evaluate, record, monitor, collect, develop, publish, authorise, schedule, determine, prepare, approve, inspect, report, decide, write, operate, update, conduct, train, review or plan.

3.13 When the action implies a judgment or decision (for example, evaluate, monitor, inspect, and review) we create a phrase to indicate the primary outcome (such as monitor stakeholder responses for information).

3.14 The activities or decisions to be made should be concise and should apply to a role or need, not to the specific person currently carrying out the task. Create a matrix with roles along the top and activities or tasks down the left side and in each of the table cells enter the appropriate RACI code.

4 Communicating with stakeholders

Keeping stakeholders informed

4.1 In today's data-rich environment, information overload is as much of a problem as lack of communication. (Just think how many useless e-mails you get in the course of a day!) Information is not exchanged with stakeholders just for the sake of it – although some non-essential communication may be helpful in building relationships and maintaining regular (non-negotiatory) contact.

4.2 It is, however, important for purchasing to keep stakeholders informed in any of the following situations.

- New information, plans or decisions are likely to affect the stakeholder's plans or interests (so that they legitimately feel they have a 'right to know'). Employees should be informed as early as possible, for example, if a plan is made to outsource activities which might cause redundancies.
- There have been changes to data, plans or decisions previously relied upon, including unforeseen contingencies (so that they 'need to know' in order to adjust their own performance). Identified schedule or cost deviations, for example, must be notified as soon as possible to those who will be affected by the overrun, and (if significant) to more senior management.
- The information represents helpful feedback to the stakeholder, enabling them to identify a problem and take corrective action, or to reinforce and celebrate positive performance (so that they are 'grateful to know': this helps to support a partnership-style relationship with suppliers, for example).

- The information is necessary to enable stakeholders to do what the organisation wants them to do (so that the organisation 'needs them to know', in order to achieve its own objectives). Customers and prospective customers need to know about products and services through advertising, for example, in order to be persuaded to purchase – and suppliers need to know about supply needs, specifications and contract terms in order to fulfil them.

4.3   In some cases, the right or need to know is enshrined in law. Changes cannot be made to contract terms without due notice, for example. Employee representatives must be consulted on issues which affect their interests, under EU employee involvement provisions. In other cases, exchange of information is in both parties' best interests: suppliers will need to be informed of a proposed change to e-purchasing or EDI systems, for example, in order to support collaborative development and smooth changeover.

Communication programmes

4.4   In addition to routine stakeholder communication (such as upward reporting to a manager on a regular basis), there may be a need for a planned series of information flows or communication initiatives on a particular subject, in order to inform stakeholders, engage their interest and support (or 'buy in'), and shape their response to the information. Such a planned series of information flows is called a 'communication programme'.

4.5   Communication programmes are often planned in situations involving the management of change. Examples might include the introduction of new technology; a change of key supplier or distributor; corporate restructuring, redundancies or changes in work methods; the adoption of new purchasing policies (eg environmental or ethical standards); the launch of a new or modified product or service; or response to a potential public relations crisis (eg a product recall, environmental disaster or allegations of unethical behaviour).

4.6   You might like to stop and think who the key stakeholders are in each of these situations; what information they would need, want or expect in the situation; what information the purchasing or marketing organisation would want to give them – and for what purpose.

4.7   It is necessary to establish a formal, systematic plan for communication with stakeholders in such situations, in order to ensure that:

- The correct audience is identified and targeted (eg using stakeholder mapping to prioritise those most affected, or with most influence on the success of the plan being communicated)
- All affected stakeholders are reached with the information (ideally, at the same time, so that no-one has to find out 'by accident' from a less direct, reliable or positive source)
- Information is spread to the right people at the right time in the right way to achieve the most positive effect
- Information is spread efficiently and cost-effectively
- Information can be updated regularly where necessary
- Messages are coherent and consistent (especially important when multiple channels are being used)
- Confidential information is spread on a 'need to know' basis, and sensitive information (eg company plans and financial data) and intellectual property (eg new product designs) are protected where relevant
- Inaccurate rumours and misinformation are neutralised as far as possible
- Opportunities are given, where appropriate, to gather feedback and deal with concerns or resistance on the part of stakeholders

- The process is monitored and later reviewed, so that lessons can be learned for future communication programmes.

Why communication programmes fail

4.8 Communication programmes may fail for a number of reasons.

- Lack of planning (eg failure to identify the correct target audience; failure to ensure the consistency and coherence of messages over time; wrong timing)
- Lack of resources (eg finance, time) allocated to the programme, perhaps due to competing priorities
- Lack of opportunity for questions, concerns, arguments or suggestions to be raised by stakeholders (increasing insecurity, minimising 'ownership' and often driving resistance underground)
- Poor communication techniques: use of inappropriate media or channels; use of inaccessible language; information overload
- Lack of managerial and cultural support for the message being communicated (eg commitment not being modelled by senior management, values not being backed up by organisational policies and practices)
- Political or cultural resistance to the message, because of conflicting interests or values (eg staff not buying in to the need for restructuring or new work methods)

Stakeholder communication techniques

4.9 Stakeholder communication often involves reaching large numbers of people (or their representatives). It also often requires two-way communication: that is, opportunities for questions, concerns and views to be aired. (Being heard is important to stakeholders – just as their feedback and input is important to the organisation.) These two imperatives dictate the kinds of media and channels used in stakeholder communication programmes.

4.10 **Focus groups** are often used to gather qualitative data, views and feedback from stakeholders, particularly customers or potential customers. They consist of a group of 5–25 representatives of a target stakeholder population, together with a facilitator who encourages the group to discuss a list of relevant topics in an otherwise free and unstructured way.

4.11 This is a form of group **depth interview**, used for gathering complex qualitative information about attitudes, opinions and responses to organisational proposals and actions (such as advertising campaigns). Focus groups may be used to generate ideas for new product concepts and new products; to explore consumer responses to promotional or packaging ideas; or to conduct preliminary research into customer knowledge and opinions (which may be followed up with more extensive customer surveys, say).

4.12 Various **consultation forums** may be used to inform stakeholders about plans, and encourage the airing of questions, suggestions, concerns and feedback. In employee relations, for example, joint consultative committees or works councils may be used for discussion of issues of concern between employee (or trade union) representatives and management. Similarly, public consultation forums may be set up to allow discussion of community concerns about the environmental impacts of site developments or policy changes.

4.13 **Briefings, seminars or conferences** may be used to give information and presentations to stakeholders, and to seek feedback. These can be used on a small scale (eg team briefings, cascading information down the organisation) or on a large scale (eg the annual general meeting of shareholders, or an industry conference).

4.14 In addition to these techniques, you may be able to think of a number of others, using written and electronic (rather than face-to-face) communication. Here are some examples.

- Briefings, updates, notifications and requests for feedback delivered by email or in personalised 'standard' letters to stakeholders
- Information and updates, and feedback mechanisms, delivered via the corporate website, intranet or extranet
- Shareholder reports, delivered via mail or posted on the website, to the key target audience of shareholders and investors
- Corporate advertising and public relations, in the form of advertisements, events, exhibitions, sponsorships, press releases and so on, to various target audiences including customers and the media.

Internal stakeholder communication

4.15 Internal stakeholder communication is particularly important.

- Organisations depend on their employees (the human resources of the business) to implement plans and deliver services. Employee awareness of, engagement in and commitment to organisational goals is essential to support external customer satisfaction and business success.
- People need to work together across-functional boundaries. There therefore needs to be both systematic communication between functions, and 'internal marketing' so that different functions understand each other's needs and contributions.
- Good employee communication enhances job satisfaction, and may help to create positive 'employer brand': that is, a reputation as a good employer, which may help to attract and retain quality staff.
- Employee communication, consultation and involvement is, in many countries, provided for by law (eg in the EU, in regard to consultation about redundancies, and the use of works councils to discuss matters of concern to employees).
- Communication is a cornerstone of positive employee relations, building stable and co-operative relationships between management and employees, and minimising conflict.

4.16 Some of the methods used for employee communication include: office manuals and in-house newsletters; a corporate intranet (staff-only web pages); team meetings, briefings, presentations and conferences; bulletins and announcements on noticeboards (and their website equivalents); personalised email, letters and memoranda; day-to-day information passed on by managers to individuals and teams; and so on.

4.17 Tools which may more specifically encourage feedback or upward communication include: formal negotiating and consultative meetings (eg with employee representatives); suggestion schemes; performance appraisal interviews (where opportunities are given to discuss problems, issues and suggestions for improvement); quality circles and other consultation or discussion groups; employee attitude surveys; management participation in informal networks; and so on.

Chapter summary

- Stakeholders are often categorised as internal, connected or external.
- For purposes of stakeholder management, it is important to analyse both the power held by different stakeholder groups, and their level of interest in exercising that power. Mendelow's matrix is a formal model for doing this.
- Another framework for analysing stakeholders is Egan's 'stakeholders in change' model. Egan classifies stakeholders into nine different groups.
- The RACI model describes the various roles that are undertaken in completing tasks for a business process or project. The term stands for Responsible, Accountable, Consulted, Informed.
- It is important to keep stakeholders adequately informed, both on a routine basis, and by formal communication programmes at times when there is a particular need.

 ## Self-test questions

Numbers in brackets refer to paragraphs where you can check your answers.

1   Distinguish between internal, connected and external stakeholders. (1.2)

2   Give examples of (a) internal, (b) connected and (c) external stakeholders. (Tables 2.1, 2.2, 2.3)

3   Sketch Mendelow's matrix. What strategy should be adopted in relation to each quadrant in the matrix? (2.5, 2.6)

4   List as many as you can of Egan's nine stakeholder groups. (2.7)

5   Explain the four different roles in the RACI model. (3.6–3.9)

6   What types of exercise can the RACI model be used for? (3.11)

7   Describe situations in which it is particularly important to keep stakeholders informed. (4.2)

8   Suggest reasons why stakeholder communication programmes may fail. (4.8)

CHAPTER 3

Cross-Functional Working

Assessment criteria and indicative content

1.3 Explain the appropriateness of cross-functional working when making relationships in purchasing and supply

- Forming cross-functional teams
- The added value procurement and supply provides to cross-functional working and internal marketing
- Barriers to teamworking
- Stages of team formation
- Characteristics of successful teams

Section headings

1 Forming cross-functional teams
2 Procurement in cross-functional teams
3 Effective and ineffective teams
4 Stages of team formation

1 Forming cross-functional teams

1.1 In a 'functional' organisation structure, tasks are grouped together according to the common nature or focus of the task: production, sales and marketing, accounting and finance, purchasing and supply and so on. This enables cost-effective use of specialist expertise and related resources (eg equipment, materials, management and training relevant to that particular specialism). Unfortunately, it can also create barriers between different functions: information and work flows are primarily 'vertical' within functions, which may be seen as separate 'silos' within the organisation.

1.2 A functional organisation might be illustrated as follows: Figure 3.1.

Figure 3.1 *Functional organisation*

Cross-functional activity within organisations and supply chains

1.3 Functional organisation can be a problem because business processes – such as the flow of products through the internal supply chain – are in fact 'horizontal': work and information must flow freely across-functional boundaries, without the vertical barriers created by specialisation, departmental job demarcations and communication channels. Think about the experience of customers: they need to speak to different functions (sales, delivery, accounts, after-sales service) as they proceed through the purchase process: they don't want to know that each stage of their experience is the domain of a different department – much less that the departments don't talk to each other. Similarly, product development, quality management, partnering and learning are all horizontal activities, requiring co-operation and information exchange across-functional boundaries.

1.4 This is particularly the case with purchasing, which serves a diverse customer base, consisting of different value activities and functions. Lysons and Farrington note that, while in many organisations purchasing is a separate department responsible solely for the procurement of supplies, there is an increasing trend towards more integrated structures which take in the wider process of logistics or supply chain management: the whole sequence of activities from the acquisition of suppliers to the delivery of finished products to end-user customers. 'Such structures emphasise the importance of cross-functional decision-making', because business processes are *horizontal,* cutting across departments and disciplines: Figure 3.2.

Figure 3.2 *Business process flows across an organisation*

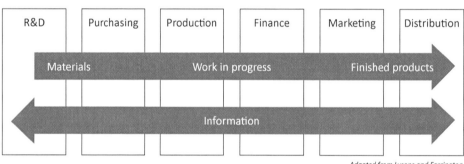

Adapted from Lysons and Farrington

1.5 Purchasing is an important link in the internal supply chain: they are the interface between other links in the chain, such as the specifiers of purchase needs, the users of the goods purchased, and the financers of the purchase – any or all of whom may be from different functional departments. Value-adding activities may be shared across different functions; co-ordination is required to develop effective 'linkages' which keep the flow of value going. For any given purchase or project, members of different functions will therefore have to work together, share information, communicate and co-ordinate their activities. Increasingly, this collaboration is structured using teams, as we will see below.

1.6 In addition, as we noted earlier, purchasing has increasingly become involved in management at a strategic level, which generally involves integrating and aligning the objectives of various functions to support the overall strategic direction of the firm.

1.7 The same kind of imperatives extend cross-functional working to *external* supply chains and networks. Different members of the supply network fulfil their own specialist functions, as sourcers or manufacturers of supplies, components or assemblies, logistics providers, marketing and advertising consultancies, distributors and so on. Supply chain relationships are therefore also cross-functional or 'cross-disciplinary', which means that there is the same need for multi-directional communication, co-ordination of effort, and sensitivity to potential barriers and differences.

Mechanisms to support cross-functional working

1.8 There has been a major trend towards more 'horizontal' structures in organisations, allowing work and information to flow more freely across-functional boundaries.

1.9 **Matrix structure** is a way of formalising cross-functional working in an organisation structure. It emerged at American aerospace company Lockheed in the 1950s, when its major customer (the US government) became frustrated at dealing separately with a number of functional specialists when negotiating defence contracts. The concept of the 'project co-ordinator' or 'customer account manager' was born.

1.10 The essence of matrix structure is dual authority: staff in different functions or regions are responsible both to their departmental managers, in regard to the ongoing activities of the department, *and* to a product, brand or account manager, in regard to activities related to that product, brand or account. This facilitates cross-functional co-operation and communication (and clear accountability) in regard to a given product or account – while at the same time ensuring that general functional activities are efficiently carried out on a day-to-day basis.

1.11 One example of a matrix structure might be to have a member of the purchasing department allocated to a particular internal customer (eg a user department) or product or brand team, with responsibility for supporting the procurement needs of that department, product or brand.

1.12 An organisation need not have a formal or complete matrix structure to take advantage of the benefits. Matrix or horizontal elements can be incorporated through more temporary, flexible mechanisms such as:

- Project management structures, with temporary project or task force teams put together to tackle particular tasks or problems, drawing on the expertise and resources of different functions and disciplines. Such structures are particularly helpful in focusing on shared objectives, in the form of specific desired outputs or results – rather than on 'business as usual' for functional participants.
- Liaison or co-ordinating positions, with facilitators ensuring that cross-functional communication and work flow occurs as required.
- Communication and information-sharing systems, such as shared-access databases, cross-functional briefings and other meetings, and email facilities. These are particularly important in 'virtual' teams and organisations, where people may be situated in different offices (or countries) and maintain collaboration solely or mainly through information and communication technology (ICT) links.
- Clearly stated shared or integrated objectives, emphasising the interdependence of different functions and the need for collaboration and information sharing in pursuit of overall corporate strategy.

1.13 The same kinds of mechanisms can be used in inter-organisational and network relationships.

Team building

1.14 Co-operative groups have been shown to be more effective than competitive groups, where individuals focused on their own contributions rather than the group's shared performance (*Deutsch*). The basic building blocks of 'team building' (creating cohesive groups) may be summarised as follows.

- Team identity: the sense of being a team (sometimes called *esprit de corps* or 'team spirit')
- Team solidarity: loyalty to the group, so that team members put in extra effort for the group and in support of its norms and values
- Commitment to shared goals: cooperation in the interests of team objectives. These may initially be team maintenance goals, but if they can be integrated with task goals (by offering the team the satisfaction of achievement, recognition or reward) the cooperative drive can be turned to the organisation's advantage
- Competition with other groups: members of a group will act in unison if the group's existence or patterns of behaviour are threatened from outside
- Positive leadership, supporting open communication, individual and team development, a trusting and co-operative team culture and so on.

1.15 Cohesion is broadly regarded as desirable in order to create committed, cooperative working, mutual loyalty and accountability, and open information sharing, all of which may help to maximise the potential synergy of teamworking *and* individual social satisfaction. However, you should be aware that it is possible for groups to become *too* cohesive. *Charles Handy* notes that 'ultra-cohesive groups can be dangerous because in the organisational context the group must serve the organisation, not itself'. If a group is completely absorbed with its own maintenance, members and priorities, it can divert energy and attention away from the task.

1.16 It can also become dangerously blinkered to outside information and feedback and may confidently forge ahead in a completely wrong direction. *I L Janis* described this as **groupthink**: 'the psychological drive for consensus at any cost, that suppresses dissent and appraisal of alternatives in cohesive decision-making groups'. Teams must be encouraged to exercise self-criticism, to welcome outside ideas and evaluations and to respond positively to conflicting evidence.

Group decision-making

1.17 Decision-making is a key team process. Team decisions may be arrived at in various ways.

- The application of authority by the leader, perhaps after taking members' views into account
- The use of power or influence, eg by a team specialist or charismatic member
- Majority rule: by voting or the leader's getting a 'sense' of the view supported by the majority of team members
- By consensus: a process whereby divergent views are examined and persuasive arguments used until there is broad agreement among all members. This takes longer, but is often more effective in implementation, as all members of the group are able to 'own' the decision.

1.18 As mentioned earlier, group decision-making tends to take longer (especially through consensus-seeking), but decisions are often better evaluated and more representative (owing to the input of different viewpoints) and therefore implemented with more commitment. In an effectively functioning group, decision-making will become less leader-centred over time: processes for constructive problem-solving will be carried out with appropriate member involvement and information sharing (without degenerating into groupthink).

Team communication

1.19 Effectively functioning groups tend to move from a leader-centred, leader-initiated pattern of communication to one where interaction is multi-directional or 'all-channel': any member can communicate directly with any other member.   Features of effective group communication therefore include:

- Open, honest communication – including the ability to deal with conflicts, issues and criticism openly, directly and fairly (without personal animosity or grudge-holding)
- Task-relevant information sharing (no withholding on a 'need to know' or 'knowledge is power' basis)
- All-member participation in meetings, discussions and decision-making. Equitable participation does not mean that all members will share *equally*, but that all members can get a fair hearing when they have something to say.
- Absence of artificial status barriers, so that senior and junior members communicate with ease.

2   Procurement in cross-functional teams

2.1   A team has been defined as 'a small group of people with complementary skills who are committed to a common purpose, performance goals and approaches for which they hold themselves jointly accountable.' (*Katzenbach & Smith*)

2.2   A team may be called together temporarily, to achieve specific task objectives (eg a project team or task force), or may be more or less permanent, with responsibilities for a particular product, product group or stage of business processes (eg a product development team). Other common uses of teamworking include: problem-solving or brainstorming groups (often used in innovation processes); quality circles (meeting regularly to discuss problems of quality, quality control and customer service in their area of work); employee representation groups (including works councils); and various committees and panels which may be convened for consultation and/or decision-making purposes. Many of these applications involve the use of cross-functional teams.

Different types of teams

2.3   Cross-functional teams comprise individuals from a range of disciplines. They may take different forms.

- *Multi-functional* or multi-disciplinary teams bring together individuals from different functional specialisms or departments, so that their competencies can be pooled or exchanged. This is often the case for product management and procurement teams, for example.
- *Multi-skilled* teams bring together a number of functionally versatile individuals, each of whom can perform *any* of the group's tasks: work can thus be shared or allocated flexibly, according to who is best placed to do a given job when required. This might be the case within a purchasing team, for example, where any member can undertake negotiations, draw up contracts, have knowledge of different categories, prepare investment appraisals and so on, as required.
- *Project* teams and task forces are short-term cross-functional teams formed for a particular purpose or outcome (eg the introduction of a just in time approach, the integration of information systems, or the review of sourcing strategies) and disbanded once the task

is complete. The members of such teams are usually seconded from various functional departments, for the duration of the team's existence, creating a matrix-type structure. However, longer-term projects (eg in the aerospace or construction industry) may require a full-time team, operating as a self-contained unit under a permanent project manager.

- *Virtual* teams are interconnected groups of people who function as a team – sharing information and tasks, making joint decisions and identifying with the team – but who are not physically present in the same location. Instead, they are linked by ICT tools such as the internet, email, 'virtual meetings' via tele-conferencing, video-conferencing or web-conferencing, shared-access databases and data tracking systems and so on.

2.4   In addition, there may be an opportunity to work in cross-organisational teams: an extension of an internal cross-functional team to include representatives of suppliers or customers. *Trent and Monczka* argue that supplier participation, in particular, can result in better information exchange; supplier support for the team's objectives; and greater supplier contribution in critical areas (eg product innovation and development).

Advantages of cross-functional teams

2.5   The basic work units of organisations have traditionally been specialised functional departments. In more recent times, organisations have adopted what *Peters and Waterman* called 'chunking': the breaking up of the organisation structure into small, flexible units, or teams. From the purchasing standpoint, teams (and particularly multi-disciplinary or cross-functional teams) have a number of advantages.

2.6   Teams facilitate the performance of tasks which require the collective skills, experience or knowledge of more than one person, discipline, function or organisation. Groups have been shown to produce better evaluated (though fewer) decisions than individuals working separately. Cross-functional teams also contribute to organisational learning, as members learn about other disciplines and work cultures. They increase team members' awareness of the 'big picture' of their tasks and decisions, by highlighting the dovetailing of different functions' objectives.

2.7   Multi-disciplinary teams facilitate the co-ordination of the work of different individuals or groups, because they bring them together across organisational boundaries, with shared goals and structured communication. This is perhaps the main reason for the increasing use of cross-functional teams in purchasing, as the 'supply chain' concept emphasises the need to deal with work flow in an integrated way, and to focus on adding value for the organisation and the customer (rather than the particular preoccupations of different functions).

2.8   Teams facilitate interactive communication and interpersonal relationships, and are thus particularly well-adapted for:

- Consulting, negotiating and conflict resolution, because they allow an interactive exchange of views and influence
- Ideas generation and encouraging creativity, because of their potential for 'bouncing' different people's ideas off each other
- Collecting and disseminating information, because of the multiple networks in which the various members are involved.

2.9   Diverse teams are useful for testing and ratifying decisions, because they represent different interests and viewpoints.

- Team decision-making may make the decision more acceptable, by taking account of a cross-section of stakeholder views. This may be important if the decision affects them and their work (for example, if they are responsible for carrying it out).
- Joint responsibility for decisions may also be important in situations where it might be risky to allow individuals to make decisions alone: if there is potential for error (due to individual inexperience or lack of knowledge, say) or even intentional fraud (due to individuals having power to make decisions unchecked by others).

2.10 Long-standing teams can offer continuity in performance and relationship management. One or more individuals may leave the organisation, but other team members remain: retaining shared knowledge and expertise, and maintaining established contacts and familiarity (eg with external customers and suppliers).

2.11 From the individual's standpoint, teams also perform some important functions.

- They satisfy social needs for friendship and belonging, mutual encouragement and support.
- They enable individuals to share the burdens of work responsibility and achieve more than they could do alone.
- They enable people to make noticeable individual contributions (which bolsters their self esteem) and at the same time to share responsibility and be part of something bigger than themselves (which bolsters their sense of security). Peters and Waterman suggest that these are the key dual needs of workers.

Problems of teamworking

2.12 However, there are some problems in using cross-functional teams. Group decision-making takes longer, especially if the group seeks to reach consensus by working through disagreements (as is the preferred style in Japan, for example). In addition, group working requires a certain amount of attention to group dynamics and group maintenance processes (not to mention numerous team meetings): this can take up time and draw energy away from the task. Group decisions may partly be based on group norms and interests – the group's own agenda – rather than the needs of the task, or indeed of the organisation.

2.13 Team decisions have also been shown to be riskier than individual decisions. Shared responsibility blurs the individuals' sense of responsibility for the outcome of the decision. Very cohesive groups, in particular, tend to protect their consensus by ignoring 'outside' information and feedback: they become blinkered and over-confident (**groupthink**). This effect is intensified by inter-group competition, which can result in dis-integration, lack of communication, and conflict between different groups.

2.14 Cross-functional teams may cause particular problems if:

- Team members are stressed or conflicted by the dual demands of a functional boss and a project leader (in a matrix structure)
- Individuals spend less time developing their own specialist expertise within their own functions, so that depth of knowledge and expertise is gradually lost.

2.15 You should also be aware that while 'teamworking' is regarded as a positive value in itself, there is such a thing as an ineffective team. Teamworking involves complex dynamics, roles and relationships and it is not easy to get it right. The important thing is not just to have teams – but to have effective teams. (We will discuss this in more detail later in the chapter.)

Teams in purchasing

2.16 Purchasers may participate in permanent or temporary (project based) cross-functional teams dealing with activities such as the implementation of particular strategies for sourcing, global sourcing or outsourcing; quality management and continuous improvement; new product or service development; investment appraisal and capital equipment buying; cost reduction programmes; research and review (eg a review of inventory levels or development of a preferred supplier list); and operational matters such as the co-ordinating of traffic with a particular supplier or distributor.

2.17 Dobler *et al* (*Purchasing & Materials Management*) note that: 'the increasing need in recent years for thorough long-range materials planning has increased the attention given to the strategic materials planning activity. A growing number of firms have... established a new planning group at the corporate level to conduct these economic and technical investigations on a continuing basis.' They cite the example of Hewlett Packard, where a group of 'commodity procurement strategy teams' is made up of members from various operating divisions and areas such as R & D, manufacturing, quality assurance and purchasing.

3 Effective and ineffective teams

What does an effective team look like?

3.1 In order to reap the potential benefits of teamworking, you need to build an effective team. What makes a team successful? Firstly, fulfilment of task and organisational goals – and, secondly, satisfied team members. According to many modern management writers, the one is not, in fact, possible without the other: satisfied team members are more likely to work in a committed and cooperative fashion towards their task objectives – while the successful achievement of task objectives actively promotes job satisfaction, in a 'virtuous' circle (as opposed to a 'vicious' circle).

3.2 There are a number of factors, both quantitative and qualitative, that might be assessed in order to decide whether or how far a team is operating effectively. Some factors cannot be taken as evidence on their own, but may suggest underlying problems in the team: accident rates, labour turnover and absenteeism, for example.

3.3 Signs of an effective team may include the following.

Quantifiable factors

- Low rate of labour turnover, accidents, absenteeism
- High output or productivity and quality performance
- Specific individual and team targets and standards are achieved
- Infrequent disruptions of work for problems, conflicts and so on

Qualitative factors

- High commitment to the achievement of targets and goals
- Clear understanding of team goals and role in organisational or supply chain activity (particularly customer care or quality)
- Clear understanding of the role of each member within the team
- Trust between members, reflected in free and open communication and the willingness to share tasks (trusting others to 'do their part')

- New idea generation and sharing of ideas
- Mutual support and facilitation by members of each other's work
- Open confrontation and investigation of problems and divergent views, with commitment to finding mutually satisfactory solutions
- Active interest and involvement in work decisions
- Seeking of opportunities for individual challenge, responsibility and development in the work.

Barriers to effective teamworking

3.4 We have focused on the attributes and dynamics of effectively maturing and functioning teams. You should be able to use the *opposite* factors to describe an ineffective or dysfunctional team. Drawing all that we've said together, the following is a brief checklist of some of the reasons identified for poor team performance.

- Lack of support, information or resources from management to fulfil the task (including lack of genuine decision-making authority and accountability)
- Physical conditions creating distance or barriers to communication and collaboration (eg geographical separation, lack of ICT links, lack of opportunities for meetings)
- Unclear or unrealistic individual or team objectives, or conflict between personal objectives ('hidden agendas') and team objectives
- Inappropriate team size (eg too large for all-member interaction) or composition (gaps or lack of balance in team roles)
- Unchecked conflicts of interest, interpersonal hostility, status barriers or the forming of sub-groups and cliques: blocking team development, co-operation and information-sharing
- Under-performing or under-motivated individuals holding back the team, and causing mistrust and resentment
- Poor team leadership, creating power conflicts and imbalances, lack of communication and uncertainty
- Unchecked team cohesion, diverting attention from the task and creating the risk of 'groupthink'
- Lack of leadership and teamworking skills to maintain team development and guide team processes (role allocation, decision-making, communication) in helpful ways
- Group norms undermining performance (eg restricting output, resisting leadership)

3.5 You can no doubt think of other factors – perhaps even from your own experience… You should also be able to think of the opposite or corrective factors which management might apply to encourage effective teamworking.

4 Stages of team formation

4.1 Teams are not static. They mature and develop. Four stages in this development were identified by *Tuckman* (1965).

4.2 **Forming** is the first stage, in which members try to find out about each other and about how the group is going to work: its purpose, composition, leadership and organisation are still being established. There will probably be a wariness about introducing new ideas: members will 'toe the line' in order not to make themselves unacceptable to the group. This cautious introductory period is essential, but not conducive to task effectiveness.

4.3 **Storming** is the second stage, in which members begin to assert themselves and test out roles, leadership, behavioural norms and ideas. There is more or less open conflict and competition around these areas – but this may also be a fruitful time, as more realistic targets are set, open communication develops and ideas are generated.

4.4 **Norming** is the real settling-down stage, in which agreements are reached about work sharing, individual requirements and output expectations. Group procedures and customs will be defined and adherence secured. The enthusiasm and brain-storming of the second stage may have died down, but methodical working can be introduced and maintained.

4.5 **Performing** is the stage at which the group focuses on executing its task: the difficulties of group development no longer distract from performance.

4.6 *Tuckman and Jensen* (1977) added further stages to the original model.

- **Dorming**: the team has been performing successfully for some time and grown complacent. It goes into a semi-automatic mode of operation, with efforts devoted primarily to the maintenance of the team itself.
- **Mourning** or **adjourning**: the team sees itself as having fulfilled its purpose, and the group disbands – either physically (eg in the case of a temporary project team) or psychologically (as the team turns to new goals, renegotiates membership roles, and returns to the forming stage for its next phase).

4.7 A group may progress through these stages quickly or slowly, may overlap stages, or may get stuck at a given stage (particularly 'storming'). The purpose of 'team building' activity is to facilitate and accelerate the development of a team towards the performing stage.

Chapter summary

- A functional structure is one in which tasks are grouped together according to the common nature of the task: production, sales and marketing, purchasing and so on.
- A problem with functional structures is that many business processes take place across-functional boundaries. This is one reason why cross-functional teams are so commonly used.
- Teams may be formed for various reasons. For example, it may be to carry out a defined project. Or it may be more permanent, with responsibilities for a particular product or stage of business processes.
- Problems associated with teamworking include groupthink, possible stress caused by dual demands, and possible loss of specialist knowledge and expertise.
- Signs of an effective team include achievement of goals and the satisfaction of team members.
- There are also significant barriers to effective teamworking, which need to be managed carefully.
- Tuckman analysed four stages in team formation: forming; storming; norming; performing. Later research added two further stages: dorming and mourning.

 ## Self-test questions

Numbers in brackets refer to paragraphs where you can check your answers.

1 Explain what is meant by a functional organisation structure. (1.1)

2 Explain what is meant by a matrix structure. (1.9)

3 List different methods by which team decisions may be arrived at. (1.17)

4 Describe different forms of cross-functional teams. (2.3)

5 List advantages of cross-functional teams. (2.5ff)

6 List quantifiable and non-quantifiable factors that indicate effective teamworking. (3.3)

7 List potential barriers to effective teamworking. (3.4)

8 Describe the stages of team formation identified by Tuckman and later research. (4.2–4.6)

CHAPTER 4

Supply Chain Relationships

Assessment criteria and indicative content

1.4 Assess the roles of personnel involved in a supply chain relationship

- Definitions of supply chain
- Examples of supply chains
- The concept of supply chain networks
- Stakeholder involvement in supply chains

Section headings

1 Definitions of supply chain
2 Examples of supply chains
3 Supply chain networks
4 Stakeholder involvement in supply chains

1 Definitions of supply chain

What is a 'supply chain'?

1.1 In a general sense, 'supply' may be defined simply as the act (or process) of providing something or making something available, often in response to buyers' or customers' requirements. It involves the transfer or flow of goods, services and information from one party to another.

1.2 The concept of the 'supply chain' can therefore be defined as follows.

- 'The supply chain includes all those involved in organising and converting materials through the input stages (raw materials), conversion phase (work in progress) and outputs (finished products). The cycle is often repeated several times in the journey from the individual producer to the ultimate customer, as one organisation's finished good is another's input.' *(Baily et al)*
- A supply chain is 'that network of organisations that are involved, through upstream and downstream linkages, in the different processes and activities that produce value in the form of products and services in the hands of the ultimate customer.' *(Christopher)*
- 'The supply chain encompasses all organisations and activities associated with the flow and transformation of goods from the raw materials stage, through to the end user, as well as the associated information flows. Material and information flows both up and down the supply chain.' *(Handfield & Nichols)*

1.3 The principal flows in a very simple supply chain are shown in Figure 4.1. In fact, as highlighted by Handfield and Nichols, it is not quite this simple: there are multiple, two-way flows along the chain. Information (in the form of enquiries, specifications, orders and delivery schedules) flows from customers *backwards* to suppliers. Then products and services (or the fulfilment of orders) flow forward through the chain, as shown in our diagram. More information (confirming receipt of the order or giving feedback) and payment then flow back again.

Figure 4.1 *Principal flows in a simple supply chain*

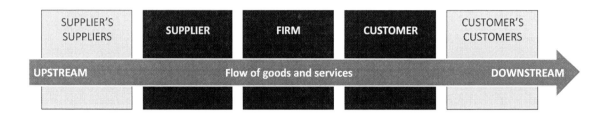

1.4 Nevertheless, we can think of the basic 'stream' as flowing from a first supplier (perhaps a raw material extractor) to a final consumer, so in relation to the firm we are focusing on (the 'focal firm'):

- Suppliers (the firms from which it *buys* the *inputs* to its activities) are said to be **upstream**; and
- Customers (the firms or individuals to whom it *sells* the *outputs* of its activities) are said to be **downstream**.

1.5 It is important for the purposes of this unit to remember that a focal firm is both a purchasing organisation (dealing with suppliers to acquire inputs to its activities) and a marketing organisation (dealing with customers to sell the outputs of its activities).

- The firm's **upstream activities** (the supply chain seen from the focal firm's perspective as a purchasing organisation) therefore include processes such as search, procurement, usage, maintenance and disposal of goods and services – and the management of relationships with suppliers.
- The firm's **downstream activities** (the supply chain seen from the focal firm's perspective as a marketing organisation) include processes such as research, design, manufacture or provision, selling and servicing of goods and services – and the management of relationships with customers.

Why think of supply as a 'chain'?

1.6 Commercial relationships – like interpersonal relationships – require at least two parties who are in contact with each other. If we focus on only two parties (for example, a single supplier and one of its customers, or a single buyer and one of its suppliers), the relationship will be a 'one to one' or 'two-party' (sometimes called 'dyadic') relationship. Some of the relationship management approaches we will be considering in this Course Book focus on this one-to-one context: Figure 4.2. How does a buying organisation ensure reliable performance by a particular supplier? How does a marketing organisation keep a particular customer happy and loyal?

Figure 4.2 *Dyadic supply relationships*

1.7 Much of the effort of purchasing professionals, as we will see, is devoted to supplier selection, development, performance management and relationship management; and the development of strategic relationships (such as partnerships and alliances) with selected suppliers of the most important goods and services. Similarly, much of the effort of marketing managers is, nowadays, devoted to developing long-term, mutually beneficial, profitable relationships with key customers or clients: a discipline often called 'relationship marketing'.

1.8 However, as we saw above, these kinds of focused supplier-customer exchanges usually happen within the context of a lengthier supply process: an extractor or producer of raw materials supplies to a processing plant or producer of components, which supplies to a manufacturing or assembly organisation, which supplies to a distributor or retail outlet, which supplies to the consumer. It is this total configuration which is often called a chain, or channel. (You may like to consider what parties and processes the supply chain would consist of, for a range of different products and services: the sort of exam question that may come up on this area of the syllabus.)

1.9 The chain metaphor highlights several useful characteristics of the supply process and relationships.

- It emphasises 'serial co-operation' or 'working together in turn': each player contributes value at its stage of the sequence of activities.
- It emphasises mutual dependency and collaboration, because each link in a chain is essential to the completeness and strength of the whole: weak links and breakages (eg an underperforming or failing supplier or distributor) may disrupt the flow of supply.
- It emphasises 'linkages' between members: value is added not just by each element in the chain, but by the quality of the relationships between them.

1.10 It is worth being aware that even this picture is simplified. In reality, each organisation in the supply chain has multiple other relationships with its own customers, suppliers, industry contacts, partners and advisers – and even competitors (in trade associations or industry think tanks, say) – any and all of whom may also be connected with each other. Many writers now argue, therefore, that a more appropriate metaphor for the supply process is not a chain, but a network or web. So even the simplest set of relationships might look something like the following: Figure 4.3.

Figure 4.3 *A simple supply network!*

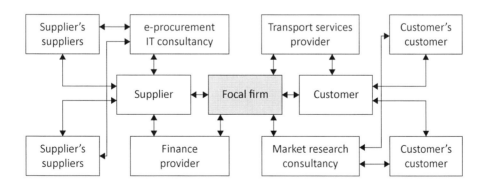

Internal and external supply chains

1.11 It is also important for the purposes of this module to realise that the supply chain concept can be applied *within* commercial organisations – as well as *between* them.

1.12 The **inter-business supply chain** describes the model we have outlined above: a linked sequence of contributors in different firms. Part or all of such a chain may be brought within the control of a single holding company. Large oil companies, for example, typically have control over all the main stages of exploration, production, refining and retailing. In most cases, however, supply chains are controlled through supply contracts and collaborative relationships between separate, independent entities. This is why client and supplier relationships are so important.

1.13 The **internal supply chain** describes a similar flow of information and other resources *within* – into and through – a given organisation: from inbound activities (purchasing and receiving inputs), to conversion activities (transforming inputs into outputs) to outbound activities (moving outputs onward to customers).

1.14 Seeing internal processes and relationships as a kind of supply chain therefore highlights the extent to which each function in an organisation acts as a link in the chain which delivers value to end customers. This is an important idea for the **internal customer concept**, which suggests that any unit of a firm whose task contributes to the task of other units can be regarded as a supplier of goods and services to those units. In order to fulfil its objectives, the supplying unit will need to anticipate and satisfy the requirements of these internal customers – just as a supplying firm will seek to do for its external customers. (You should already be familiar with the concept of internal customers from Chapter 1.)

1.15 The purchasing function is part of the internal supply chain: it is served by internal suppliers (for example, the finance function which provides budgetary reports and finance allocations, and the technical department which provides specifications and requisitions) and in turn serves internal customers (the various other functions on whose behalf it procures supplies, or to whom it gives advice).

2 Examples of supply chains

Differences in supply chains

2.1 It is useful to consider the differences that may arise in the supply chain of an organisation. This is particularly of interest in connection with the means by which organisations sell their products. A useful distinction is between organisations that supply consumer products and those that sell industrial products.

2.2 The differences in the supply chains of such organisations are illustrated in Figure 4.4.

Figure 4.4 *Consumer and industrial supply chains*

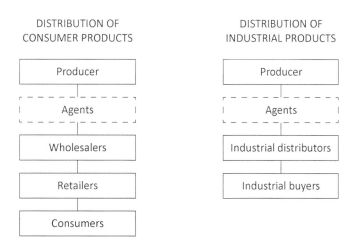

2.3 The use of agents depends very much on normal practice within the industry sector, as indicated by the dotted lines in Figure 4.4.

2.4 Figure 4.4 illustrated the downstream distribution of a producer's goods to the eventual customers. We might equally illustrate the upstream supply chain: see Figure 4.5.

Figure 4.5 *Example of an upstream supply chain*

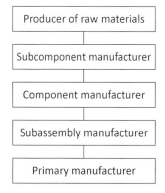

2.5 In a retail environment, the supply chain looks very different. See Figure 4.6, which is due to Baily *et al* in *Purchasing Principles and Management*.

Figure 4.6 *Supply chains in retailing*

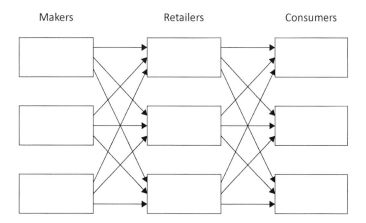

3   Supply chain networks

Supply networks or webs

3.1   Many writers (such as *Cox and Lamming,* and *Christopher)* argue that the chain metaphor should be replaced by that of a network or web. The firm is in fact linked to multiple players, both upstream and downstream. And any given supplier or customer is also likely to be linked to *other* firms in its own roles as supplier, customer or competitor: suppliers usually do not provide exclusively to one customer. This more complex set of interrelated transactions and contacts can be depicted as a network

3.2   The contribution of the network metaphor can be summarised as follows.

- It is a more strategic model for mapping and analysing supply chain relationships, and therefore for seeking to exploit synergies and improve performance in innovative, systemic and responsive ways.
- It raises the possibility of a wider range of collaborations (eg supplier associations, buying consortia or strategic alliances) which may offer mutual advantages – and perhaps alter the balance of power in supply relationships.
- It represents both 'nodes' (activities or facilities that add value to the supply chain) and the links (transfers or flows) between them.
- It recognises the potential of 'extended enterprises' and virtual organisations: extending the strategic capability of the firm through the collective resources and performance of network contributors.
- It recognises that extended enterprises may overlap (with particular suppliers or customers in common), creating complex patterns of relationship, competition and potential risk (eg to information and intellectual property).

Supply pipelines, channels and rivers

3.3   Supply chains are also sometimes referred to as pipelines or channels, emphasising that they provide a containing structure for flows of materials, goods, information and so on. (Downstream activities are often referred to in this way: distribution channels, channel management and so on.)

3.4   This analogy also helpfully raises 'push' and 'pull' issues: whether flows are driven by supply-side (push) or demand-side (pull) factors. Push marketing strategies, for example, are aimed at trade promotion (getting goods into the front end of the pipeline by selling to distributors and retailers), while pull strategies are aimed at stimulating consumer demand (stimulating flow by drawing goods out of the pipeline at the other end). *Emmett* suggests that the water supply analogy specifically raises the demand-driven nature of supply, as goods are required, as it were, 'on tap'.

3.5   The metaphor of the river emphasises the flow nature of supply, and provides the terminology 'upstream' (flowing to a given point) and 'downstream' (flowing from a given point). It reflects the holistic nature of the flow, not distinguishing particular points or players within it, and its constant direction towards the customer.

Internal supply chains

3.6 *Harland* (1996) identifies four ways in which the term 'supply chain' can be understood: internal supply chains, dyadic supply relationships, inter-business chains, and inter-business networks.

3.7 The internal supply chain (or value chain) describes the processes which integrate all the business functions and units responsible for the flow of materials and information into and through the organisation. Consider the sequential flow of materials, information and eventually finished goods from purchasing to goods inwards, inspection, storage, production, inspection (finished goods), storage (finished goods) and transport or distribution.

3.8 Viewing internal processes as a supply chain in their own right highlights aspects such as process alignment (and the need for horizontal work and information flows), the internal customer concept and Porter's value chain concept (which is specifically intra-firm in focus).

Dyadic supply relationships

3.9 Dyadic supply relationships are direct two-sided relationships between customers and suppliers. As discussed earlier, this used to be the main way in which supply chains were viewed, focusing on how the firm could secure and exploit the technical contribution of its immediate upstream suppliers, and what it could offer to its immediate downstream customers.

3.10 Despite the trend towards a wider supply chain concept, the management of a firm's immediate upstream and downstream relationships is still important, as reflected in approaches such as supplier relationship management (SRM) and customer relationship management (CRM). Much of the effort of purchasing managers is devoted to supplier selection, development, performance management and relationship management (particularly vital where services or operations have been outsourced); and the development of strategic relationships (such as partnerships and alliances) with selected suppliers.

3.11 You should be able to recognise the dyadic focus of a wide range of purchasing management techniques: vendor managed inventory, early supplier involvement, vendor rating and so on.

Inter-business networks

3.12 Inter-business networks describe the various interrelationships of suppliers (and their own customer and competitor networks) and customers (and own their supplier and competitor networks). As we noted earlier, this embraces more complex views of the extended and virtual enterprise.

3.13 *Martin Christopher* suggests that the development of supply networks poses three major challenges for organisations.

- The need to view strategy development as a collective process, seeking competitive advantage for the whole marketing network (focused on consumer value and satisfaction), rather than individual players.
- The need to develop win-win thinking: being prepared to let go of a competitive, distributive or zero-sum mindset in buyer-supplier relations, in order to explore options for mutual advantage. The aim is to 'expand the pie' (by collaboratively creating value), so that even competitive gain-sharing results in a win for all parties.
- The need for open communication: sharing information in order to facilitate collaborative

efficiency, co-ordination, flexibility and innovation. This may involve a degree of transparency (eg on costs, cost structures, expectations, ideas) that requires mutual trust.

4 Stakeholder involvement in supply chains

Defining stakeholders: a recap

4.1 As we have seen, 'Stakeholders are those individuals or groups who depend on the organisation to fulfil their own goals and on whom, in turn, the organisation depends.' (Johnson & Scholes)

'A stakeholder of a company is an individual or group that either is harmed by, or benefits from, the company *or* whose rights can be violated, or have to be respected, by the company.' (Jobber)

4.2 From these definitions, you might note that the members (managers and employees) of an organisation are stakeholders in its activity and success. So are its supply chain partners (suppliers, intermediaries and customers) and others in direct business relationship with it (such as its owners or shareholders, the banks that lend it money and so on). An organisation therefore has both *internal* and *external* stakeholders.

4.3 The group of external stakeholders is, however, wider than you might think. It includes a number of parties who are not directly connected to the organisation, but who contribute to its activities, or are impacted on *by* its activities, in some way. They include the government, pressure groups and interest groups (including professional bodies and trade unions), the news media, the local community and wider society.

4.4 An organisation negotiates legal (and psychological) contracts with its employees, financers and supply chain partners – but why should it enter into any kind of relationship with these more peripheral groups? Stakeholder theory recognises that an organisation affects its environment and is affected by its environment. Each of the secondary stakeholder groups mentioned may contribute something to the organisation, or exert some kind of influence over it; and each may be affected (positively or negatively) by its plans and activities. The concept of corporate social responsibility argues that organisations should, as Jobber's definition suggests, respect the rights of such groups where possible.

4.5 You may also be asked to focus on the stakeholders of a particular function (such as procurement) or of a particular project, plan or decision (eg stakeholders in a project to implement e-procurement or a decision to offshore production). From this point of view, the key internal stakeholders of procurement would be those functions and groups within the organisation who impact on, or are impacted by, procurement activity. Its key external stakeholders would be shareholders, suppliers, financers, service providers and so on.

Stakeholder relationship management

4.6 Because stakeholders may have an interest in influencing organisational (or procurement) decisions – and may have the power to do so – it is important to:

- Take their interests and likely responses into account
- Communicate effectively with them on matters that affect them
- Engage the interest, support and commitment of influential (and potentially helpful) groups
- Manage potential issues and problem areas that might arouse resistance or opposition from influential groups.

4.7   As with customers and suppliers, stakeholder management for wider stakeholders will involve: gathering information about groups and their interests; prioritising groups which have most potential impact; ensuring consistent and coherent communication with them; establishing opportunities for co-operation and synergy (where available); and continuously monitoring, evaluating and adjusting the relationship over time.

4.8   The key point is to recognise the wider 'web' of relationships in which an organisation (or procurement function) may need to be involved – both internally and externally – and the wider interests which it will need to take into account, in order to ensure both business effectiveness and ethical responsibility.

4

Chapter summary

- A supply chain consists of a number of organisations linked together by virtue of being customers and suppliers to each other.
- A more realistic (less simplified) metaphor is a supply network. This is a more strategic model for mapping and analysing supply relationships.
- It is also possible to speak of an internal supply chain, recognising that a function such as purchasing performs tasks to benefit other functions (internal customers) within the organisation.
- Supply chains have stakeholders. Indeed, all members of a supply chain are stakeholders in the chain.
- It is important to manage relationships with supply chain stakeholders.

 ## Self-test questions

Numbers in brackets refer to paragraphs where you can check your answers

1   Define 'supply chain'. (1.2)

2   What is meant by a dyadic supply relationship? (1.6)

3   Describe what is meant by an internal supply chain. (1.13)

4   Sketch a simple supply network in the retailing sector. (Figure 4.6)

5   What characteristics of supply relationships are brought out by the network metaphor? (3.2)

6   According to Martin Christopher, what three challenges are posed by the development of supply networks? (3.13)

7   List possible steps in the management of supply chain stakeholders. (4.6)

CHAPTER 5

An Introduction to Marketing

Assessment criteria and indicative content

2.1 Review the principles and definitions of marketing
- The marketing concept
- Market driven approaches compared to product or sales led approaches

Section headings

1 The marketing concept
2 Organisational orientations

1 The marketing concept

Development of the marketing concept

1.1 Marketing is not a new theory; it has simply not been approached academically until relatively recently. It is only in the last 30 or 40 years that we have started to recognise consumption as being the sole purpose of production. Think about the subject. What do you understand by the term marketing? It is a difficult term to define yet most of us use the word frequently.

1.2 This section looks at the history of marketing and then provides definitions. By the end of the chapter you will understand the basis of marketing, as required by your syllabus.

1.3 Trade has existed from the very early days of civilisation. Imagine the early cavemen exchanging meat for wood to make a fire. Both parties in this exchange process were able to benefit from trading with each other. Trade today is in principle similar to this except that we normally exchange goods for money rather than for other goods (although this is not always the case).

1.4 The Industrial Revolution (approximately 1730–1850) transformed Britain from a mainly agricultural country to a predominantly industrial one. In the Western world, it produced changes in all aspects of people's lives: politics, art, religion, literature, morals and, with the rise of democracy, social reforms.

1.5 Before the industrial revolution production was usually on a small scale. During the industrial revolution production became organised into much larger units and towns developed. Trade grew as people started to purchase goods for their own consumption rather than producing the goods themselves. In course of time, this trend spread beyond Britain and the West. Nowadays, developed and developing economies are to be found across the whole world.

1.6 Because of this trend there was a major change in trade. Buyers no longer had contact with sellers and it therefore became necessary for producers to find out what buyers wanted. Bear in mind that because of mass production the number and types of products available for trade increased dramatically.

1.7 Sellers concentrated on production techniques in order to lower costs. The aim at this early stage was to sell the products that were produced, whatever they happened to be. It was not until relatively recently that companies began to recognise the need to satisfy customers.

1.8 The concept of marketing is based on putting the customer first: finding out what customers want and giving it to them. It seems obvious now that if you don't give a customer what he wants, you will not be in business for long.

1.9 Customer satisfaction is the main principle in marketing. It is that simple, and all strategic thinking and concepts that we will discuss in this chapter have the main aim of keeping the customer happy.

Current definitions of marketing

1.10 We have seen that marketing is a relatively simple concept but, because it has only recently been studied in academic spheres, and because the practice of marketing is much more complex than the principles, theorists have developed numerous definitions.

1.11 We will look at a few of these definitions so that you can see the scope of the subject. It is likely that you will want to use at least one during the examination. The definition given by the UK Chartered Institute of Marketing (CIM) is probably the one most used.

1.12 According to the CIM 'Marketing is the management process responsible for identifying, anticipating and satisfying customer requirements profitably'. You can see that the CIM brings in the concept of making a profit while satisfying customers. It is a logical progression: if you give customers what they want, you can hope to make a profit in the process.

1.13 The definition also implies that organisations should be proactive in their search for products and services which will satisfy customers. This proactive approach will lead to **anticipation of customer requirements**.

1.14 Perhaps the drawback of the CIM definition is that it does not cover the case of non-profit organisations. It states that marketing is concerned with making a profit. This might lead you to think about the case of non-profit organisations and how the marketing concept applies. Does a charity need to think about marketing? Does a hospital need to think about marketing?

1.15 Another definition of marketing by Philip Kotler is that it is 'a social and managerial process by which individuals and groups obtain what they need and want through creating and exchanging products and value with others'.

1.16 Kotler's definition of marketing talks about the exchange process. As discussed earlier, this is the basis of all trade. He does not mention profit but instead talks about 'value' which means the benefits to all parties involved in the exchange process.

1.17 A cliché that summarises the whole marketing concept is that marketing is about selling goods that don't come back to customers who do.

1.18 Marketing can be viewed as an organisational function, a business concept and an organisational philosophy.

- Marketing – like purchasing, finance etc – is an organisational function, staffed by people with relevant skills, and tasked with certain responsibilities.

- Marketing is a business concept that has been developed and, increasingly, analysed over the last few decades. We have discussed this point above.
- Marketing is an organisational philosophy based on the need above all to anticipate and satisfy customer needs. We will contrast this view of marketing with other business 'orientations' later in this chapter.

1.19 The key points that you need to remember from this discussion are as follows.

- Marketing focuses attention on the needs and wants of customers.
- Marketing is about satisfying needs and wants.
- Marketing involves all decisions being made with careful consideration of customers.
- Marketing can be viewed as a process in which organisations deliver solutions to customers' problems.

2 Organisational orientations

Introduction

2.1 We know that marketing is a relatively new concept and even today many organisations tend to ignore its principles. Among commercial businesses we can distinguish four types of orientation: production orientation, product orientation, sales orientation and marketing orientation. We will look at these in turn so that we can gain a better understanding of the marketing concept.

Production and product orientation

2.2 The advent of the industrial revolution caused many businesses to see production as the sole purpose for their existence. Demand for products was high and so businesses tended to focus on the process of producing more goods at lower cost.

2.3 Their basic business philosophy involved identifying products that they wanted to produce and that they could produce well, rather than identifying customers' requirements. It may seem hard to believe, but many organisations operate with this orientation today. Some manufacturers focus their attention on existing products and pay little attention to the changing needs and wants of their customers.

2.4 **Product orientation** is a short-sighted view and assumes that as long as the products are excellent, customers will want them. Customers then have to be informed of the products and convinced of their superiority. This task will fall on the sales force. But customers may be looking for a different kind of product to satisfy their need – no matter how perfectly manufactured a product may be, it will still be rejected by customers if a more suitable answer to their need is developed by someone else.

2.5 In a **production-orientated** business, which focuses on the effectiveness of the production process, senior personnel will probably come from production backgrounds. The marketing function may not even exist within the organisation. Often, products are produced in a way that ensures maximum 'efficiency' in the organisation, without regard to whether customers want to buy them.

2.6 You might well agree that it is important for firms to produce only good products which they are good at producing. This may be the case, but a business must also ensure that customers want the products. This is the primary difference between production or product orientation and marketing orientation. If a business is marketing-orientated, it will produce products because customers want them. It will find efficient and effective ways to produce these desired products.

2.7 Despite this, there are cases where a production orientation may be appropriate. One such case is where demand exceeds supply: manufacturers must then look to increase production levels. Another case is where a product's price is too high: manufacturers must then look to improve production efficiency in order to produce the goods economically.

Sales orientation

2.8 A sales-orientated business assumes that demand can be created through the use of effective sales techniques. It is the sales department who are the most important people in the organisation.

2.9 In historical terms, sales orientation followed after production orientation but many sales-orientated companies exist today. A familiar example is double-glazing companies who are traditionally associated with the 'hard-sell'.

2.10 Sales orientation is a step forward from production orientation because at least managers realise that products will not sell themselves. They look for means to differentiate their products so that customers do not select competitors' offerings.

2.11 A common mistake is to assume that marketing is about sales and promotions. It is not. Selling and promoting is only one aspect of marketing and does not always consider customer satisfaction. Instead it relies on the use of sales techniques to induce customers to buy more. It uses sales techniques to overcome customers' resistance to purchase. Although businesses of this kind will initially be profitable, they are not ensuring a long-term existence. Customers will not purchase the same products from the same company again, if they have been unhappy with their first purchase.

2.12 Again you might agree that all businesses have to sell in order to be profitable. This is true. However it is the purpose of selling that is the differentiating issue. A marketing-orientated business will sell only those goods that will lead to the customer being satisfied. This technique will ensure repeat sales.

Marketing orientation

2.13 It should be clear by now that marketing is about customers and sometimes we refer to marketing orientation as customer orientation.

2.14 Marketing orientation is a long-term view. The emphasis is on finding out what customers want. The marketing orientated business will then produce goods and services that satisfy customer requirements. What managers must remember is that customers have a choice not only in the products they buy, but in the suppliers they buy those products from. To beat competitors and ensure a customer returns again and again, marketing orientation is the only viable option.

2.15 Marketing involves the whole organisation. The organisation must have a 'company-wide' philosophy based on customer requirements. Because of this, senior management within organisations must be committed to the concept. Figure 5.1 displays the differences between a marketing and a selling orientation.

Figure 5.1 *The selling and marketing concepts contrasted*

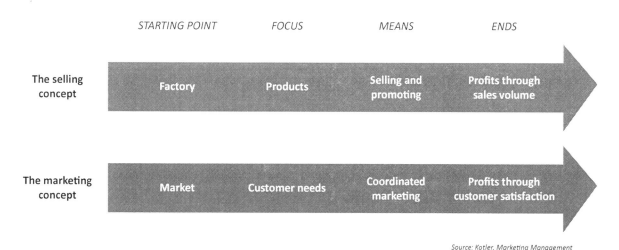

Source: Kotler, Marketing Management

2.16 The figure indicates that the starting point for marketing orientated businesses is the market (customer) whereas the starting point for a sales-orientated company is the factory. It is this point which causes the major differences between the two approaches.

Achieving a marketing orientation

2.17 Marketing should be the organisation's whole approach and business philosophy but it should also be a management or functional area as well. It should play a coordinating role with other functions in the organisation.

2.18 The position of marketing as a management function is indicated in the CIM definition that we discussed earlier. As a function, marketing should be managed similarly to other functional areas. It will take part in strategic planning and use appropriate tools to achieve departmental objectives. These tools will be discussed later in the text but for reference are known collectively as the **marketing mix**.

2.19 The coordinating role of marketing for a marketing orientated organisation is of primary importance. Marketing must be coordinated with every other department so that all employees understand the importance of the customer. It is of little use if the marketing department carries out research and produces products that the customer wants but the receptionist is impolite to customers who phone with queries. So, a marketing orientation implies a business where every employee recognises the importance of the customer.

2.20 This coordination does not always exist in practice, as you may recognise from your own organisation or others that you deal with. Too often, marketing departments operate in isolation with little communication with other departments. They make decisions which will affect the whole organisation, but do not take into consideration the effect of such decisions. The relationship between marketing and other functions, requires careful coordination if the marketing philosophy is to be followed by the whole company.

2.21 To summarise, marketing involves the whole organisation in thinking about and aiming towards customer satisfaction. The result of this philosophy will be an organisation that survives into the long term through repeat purchasing from customers. It is this long-term perspective which distinguishes the marketing-orientated business. Marketing personnel will have senior positions within the organisation structure if a marketing orientation is pursued.

Chapter summary

- There are many definitions of marketing but all revolve around the customer.
- The focus of many organisations in recent years has been on long-term customer satisfaction and developing a marketing orientation.
- Organisations still exist that operate either a production or sales orientation.
- Marketing operates as a function, a business concept and a philosophy within an organisation.

Self-test questions

Numbers in brackets refer to the paragraphs where you can check your answers.

1   Give one definition of marketing. (1.12–1.15)

2   Summarise the key issues of the marketing concept. (1.19)

3   Why did production orientation develop? (2.2)

4   What is a marketing orientation? (2.14)

5   How does marketing orientation differ from sales orientation? (2.15)

6   Why must marketing play a coordination role in an organisation? (2.19)

CHAPTER 6

The Marketing Mix

Assessment criteria and indicative content

2.2 Explain techniques associated with marketing

- The 4Ps and 7Ps approaches to marketing
- The marketing mix
- Market segmentation
- Market targeting

Section headings

1 The 4Ps of marketing
2 The 7Ps of marketing
3 Market segmentation and market targeting

1 The 4Ps of marketing

The role of marketing

1.1 It is the role of marketing to apply various techniques and tools so as to achieve marketing objectives, which in turn assist and support overall corporate objectives. The idea is to implement a marketing orientation within the organisation.

1.2 The main areas in which the marketing function is active are sometimes referred to collectively as the marketing mix.

The marketing mix

1.3 The recognised tools available to a company in order to apply the marketing concept are the elements of the marketing mix. These elements are controllable; in other words, decisions about these elements are within the direct control of the organisation or the marketing manager. They can be used to achieve departmental as well as organisational objectives. The elements of the marketing mix are as follows.

- Product
- Price
- Place
- Promotion.

1.4 Often these elements are known as the 4Ps.

1.5 The word 'place' might have little meaning to you. It simply refers to distribution, ie the methods used to get products to customers.

1.6 It is the marketing mix which is the basis of all marketing decisions. We will introduce each of these elements now so that you have an overview of them. You should learn the elements of the marketing mix as they are continually used in marketing.

1.7 The 4Ps are used in combination. They should be coordinated with each other in order to form a full impression on the customer. For example, the image of a Rolls Royce car would severely deteriorate if it was priced the same as a Ford Ka. A Rolls Royce is hardly promoted at all and the customer often has to seek a dealer to purchase it from. It is the combination of the four elements that create the image a Rolls Royce has.

1.8 It is vitally important to combine and coordinate each element of the marketing mix. All four elements contribute to the image the customer will have of the company and its products.

1.9 While the marketing mix is essentially controllable, decisions around it are not taken in isolation. A company must bear in mind external and environmental factors when it takes any decisions.

Product

1.10 In marketing terms, the product is anything which you sell to your customers. Therefore, a product can be a tangible object or an intangible service. Generally, product strategy involves developing the right good or service for a company's customers.

1.11 Decisions around the product relate to the following matters.

- Product line to be offered
- Quality, design, and content of products
- The customers to sell to
- Quantities of products to be sold
- Research and development of new products
- Brand names
- Packaging
- Warranties
- Associated services

1.12 You can see that there are an unlimited number of possibilities for decisions on the product. Again, it is emphasised that product decisions are not made in isolation. They are decisions that should be combined with other elements of the marketing mix.

Price

1.13 The pricing element of the marketing mix is critical. All other elements of the mix are costs, but this element brings money into the organisation. It is difficult to price a product correctly and a lot of options are available to the marketer.

1.14 Pricing is a complex issue and can be closely scrutinised by both customers and competitors. It requires thorough research before decisions are taken.

1.15 Pricing alternatives include the following.

- Premium or bargain pricing
- Credit policies
- Discounts

- Pricing margins to be achieved
- Competitive pricing
- Premiums
- Quantity offers

1.16 As usual, price should be considered in relation to the other marketing mix elements. For example, a pair of plastic shoes cannot be premium priced because they are usually seen as a low quality product. The price and quality perception in the customer's mind will be confused.

1.17 Another example of the relationship of price to product can be displayed in the use of branding. Should a company decide that its products will be branded, then this will influence the pricing decisions. Think about the price of Calvin Klein jeans. Because of the strength of the Calvin Klein brand, customers are willing to pay a premium price for the jeans.

Place

1.18 As we have already discovered, place refers to distribution. Distribution is the means by which companies make their goods available to customers.

1.19 Distribution considerations include the following.

- Channels between company and customer (agents, retailers etc)
- Management of channels
- Stock levels
- Delivery
- Transportation
- Warehousing
- Physical distribution

1.20 Distribution decisions should be coordinated with other marketing mix decisions. If we use the Rolls Royce example again, you can see that the image of the Rolls Royce would suffer if there was a Rolls Royce dealer on every corner. This is an example of why an organisation is not always concerned with achieving the highest distribution levels possible.

Promotion

1.21 Often, the promotion element of the marketing mix is the one which everyone recognises – so much so that people assume that marketing is promotion. In fact though promotion is only one element of the marketing mix and is of no more or less importance than any other element of the mix.

1.22 The reason why promotion is recognised and assumed to be the major thrust of marketing is that it is conspicuous. We see advertisements every day, whereas development of new products is not so obvious.

1.23 Promotion in marketing is also known as communication because it is the only area of marketing which is used to communicate directly with customers.

1.24 Methods of promotion include the following.

- Advertising – media selection, frequency, timing, content
- Sales promotion – special offers, competitions, 'buy one get one free', coupons etc

- Personal selling – the management and motivation of the salesforce
- Publicity – public relations, image management

1.25 Once again, we emphasise that the promotional element of the marketing mix works in conjunction with the other elements. If we think about the Rolls Royce example, you would seriously question the image of a Rolls Royce if it was advertised on television regularly or if a sales representative called at your door trying to sell one to you.

1.26 It is clear that marketing is a functional area of management which utilises the marketing mix to achieve both marketing and corporate objectives. Figure 6.1 summarises the marketing mix.

Figure 6.1 *The marketing mix*

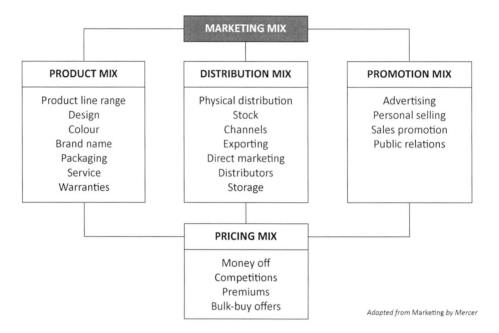

Adapted from Marketing *by Mercer*

1.27 You can see from this diagram that the elements in the marketing mix are interdependent and together create a complete image of the product or service that is being sold.

2   The 7Ps of marketing

The growth of the service sector

2.1 In recent years there has been huge growth in the service sectors of developed economies. In many cases the provision of services in such economies exceeds the provision of manufactured items.

2.2 There are a number of reasons for this trend.

- An increase in the general level of individual prosperity within developed economies. Services that people would previously have managed without, or would have performed for themselves, are now affordable purchases from dedicated suppliers. This is particularly noticeable in the household sector (for example, more people now employ part-time cleaners, gardeners etc). The trend is accentuated by the number of women nowadays in employment; they have less time to perform such services for themselves, and more money to pay others.
- An increase in leisure time. Suppliers such as restaurants, tour operators etc specialise in helping people to fill their leisure time with pleasurable pursuits.

- Increased complexity of people's lives. People indulge in a large number of pursuits that previously would have been the preserve of a privileged minority. For example, in a developed economy most people will be managing a variety of financial products (bank accounts, stock-market investments etc). This gives rise to a need for specialist advisers.
- Advances in technology. Not only do technological advances increase the types of service that can be offered, but also the use of technology itself requires organisations that can service the technology.

What is a service?

2.3 Although a service is treated similarly to a product in marketing terms, it does have distinguishing features. Also, the after-sales service provided by a selling organisation is part of the augmented product. We will look at these features only briefly. Services have the following characteristics and features.

- Intangibility: a service cannot be tasted, touched, seen or smelled before it is purchased. For instance, you will not see the results of going to the dentist before you purchase the service. Because of this a customer will look for other evidence of the service quality, such as the price, the promotional material, the location and the staff who provide the service.
- Inseparability: services are produced and consumed at the same time. A service cannot be stored. Using our dentist example again, we can see that both the patient and the dentist have to be present for the service to be provided. Therefore, the influence, personality and performance of the staff providing the service is paramount to success.
- Heterogeneity: the quality of a service will be variable. Because of inseparability, the service will be influenced by many factors such as the patient's mood, the dentist's mood, the weather etc. So, it is difficult for a customer to be sure of the outcome of any service he participates in. This is different from buying a tangible product mass-produced on a production line: in this case, it is likely that one unit from the production process is indistinguishable from another.
- Perishability: a service cannot be stored so supply of a service is difficult to control. For instance, a dentist cannot store the service of filling a tooth. He may find demand high on some days while there are no patients on other days. The result of this is that the dentist must always have the capacity to meet high levels of demand, which will be costly during slower periods.

Elements in the extended marketing mix

2.4 The result of these distinguishing characteristics is that services marketing can be quite complex. Because of this the marketing mix is extended beyond the traditional four elements (product, price, place and promotion) to seven elements. The additional three elements in the **extended marketing mix** are people, process and physical evidence, as detailed below. We therefore refer to the 7Ps of the extended marketing mix.

2.5 **People** refers to the actual employees delivering the service. Customer satisfaction can often depend on the person providing the service, because the service is inseparable from the person delivering it. If the employee is inefficient or poorly motivated then interaction with the customer will be affected. It is for this reason that organisations which provide services must be aware of the importance of their 'people'. Attention should be given to recruitment and selection, staff training and motivation in order to minimise heterogeneity of the service.

6

2.6 People are a crucial element in service delivery, since services generally take the form of activities performed by people for or on behalf of others. The service quality depends completely on the competence and attitude of the person performing it. This means that effective customer service depends on:

- Leadership, organisation culture, direction and supervision emphasising customer focus and service quality
- The recruitment, selection, appraisal, reward and disciplining of staff with customer service at the heart of performance criteria
- The training, development and motivation of staff to foster customer service competencies and attitudes
- Organisational structures supportive of customer service: empowering front-line staff to make decisions (within sensible guidelines) to solve customer problems; facilitating 'horizontal' communication to solve customer problems across departmental barriers; and supporting teamworking.

2.7 **Process** refers to the methods used to provide the service. Procedures for dealing with customers and for supplying the service must be carefully planned and managed to minimise heterogeneity. Many organisations have moved to computerised switchboards to achieve this. Because staff are not involved the customer receives the same standard of service every time he calls the organisation. Additionally, processes must be in place to ensure that the service is provided efficiently during peak hours. For instance, a hairdresser might employ Saturday staff because this is the busiest day of the week. Because a service is perishable the hairdresser will lose custom if he cannot meet demand.

2.8 Processes include the policies, procedures and systems that support service delivery, sometimes called 'back office' systems. They are particularly important in service delivery, because services are otherwise so difficult to standardise: they differ according to who is delivering them, when and in what circumstances. Services also happen in real time – they can't be pre-made and stored in advance of demand – so it is essential to have processes in place to anticipate and meet demand, and avoid customers having to wait.

2.9 Some key process requirements include the following.

- Specifying services and service levels
- Establishing policies and programmes for customer care
- Implementing procedures for efficiency and standardisation of service
- Automating or computerising services (eg ticketing), for consistency, accuracy and speed, or to empower customers for self-service
- Streamlining processes, or planning for the flexible allocation of resources (eg co-ordinating staffing levels to meet demand), to cut down queuing and waiting times
- Developing and integrating information systems, for information gathering, processing and communication, both internally (to support horizontal service delivery) and at 'touch points' with the customer (eg by integrating telephone and computer systems for customer 'recognition' and real-time access to transaction and account details)
- Capacity management, matching supply to demand in a timely and cost-effective way
- Improving the accessibility of facilities, premises, personnel and services: eg implementing 24/7 customer contact through call centres or message services; improving horizontal communication within organisations to improve access to purchasing staff when needed; improving store layouts to improve customer access to facilities and so on

- Empowering customers for self service (eg self collection and assembly of IKEA furniture, online self-service travel ticketing) and/or choice of service elements and levels (eg delivery options)
- Monitoring and gathering feedback on customer service and customer satisfaction, with a view to continuous improvement and problem-solving. One important aspect of this is customer complaint procedures.

2.10 **Physical evidence** can be used to overcome the problems of intangibility. The marketer must provide evidence of the level of quality his company offers to entice the customer. This can be provided through:

- brochures
- fixtures and fittings
- facilities
- equipment in use
- staff uniforms.

2.11 Physicals are the tangible evidences of a service having been purchased and delivered, and tangible aspects of the service environment which are part of the whole 'package' of service. This is particularly important, because of the intangibility of services, and the fact that the customer doesn't end up *owning* anything as part of the service itself: it is difficult for customers to perceive, evaluate and compare the qualities of service provision, or to feel that they have received anything meaningful for their money. Physical elements may include:

- Physical evidence of the service and the benefits it confers: tickets (for booking services), vouchers (to prove that a future service has been purchased), receipts and invoices, information brochures, follow-up confirmation letters or emails, customer loyalty, discount or credit cards and so on
- Physical features built into the design and specification of the service or service environment: the décor and ambience of the premises; the smartness of staff uniforms; the use of logos to identify service staff; name badges or business cards to help customers identify servers; and so on.

3   Market segmentation and market targeting

Definitions

3.1 Segmentation is defined by Schiffman and Kanuk (in *Consumer Behaviour*) as 'the process of dividing a potential market into distinct subsets of consumers with common needs or characteristics'. Target marketing is a process by which marketers segment their markets, as in this definition, decide on which segments to aim for (rather confusingly called 'market targeting'), and then design products and marketing campaigns tailored to each segment of interest (called 'product positioning'). This three-stage process is analysed in greater depth later in this chapter.

3.2 In more simple terms, segmentation involves dividing a total market into distinct groups of customers who share common characteristics. For example, any consumer market can be divided into two by looking at male and female purchasers as separate subsets. Such subsets are known as segments. In reality, segmentation is quite scientific and segments can be much more specific than the example just used. This will become more obvious when we discuss the variables used in the segmentation process.

3.3 Before we go any further it is important to understand the meaning of the word 'market'. It is a word that is used very frequently but often incorrectly. A market consists of both current and potential customers with the ability to buy a product or service. A person wishing to buy a car may not form part of the market for a dealer in Mercedes if he is not able to afford a luxury model.

3.4 The purpose of segmenting markets according to common characteristics is that customers in the same segment will have similar needs and wants. Based on this, customers in the same segment should display similar buying behaviour and purchase similar products and services. Segments can then be approached using a 'targeted' marketing mix strategy. The alternative to this is mass marketing where a company mass produces and mass promotes one product for all customers. Although cost effective, you can see that this is virtually impossible in consumer markets because of the diversity of needs and wants.

3.5 In an ideal world, each market segment would consist of one person. This would enable companies to be totally marketing orientated as they would be able to satisfy every individual. Unfortunately this is not a profitable way of doing business. Instead, marketers group each of us, as individuals, into segments. In marketing terms, you are not an individual. You are a member of various segments of the population. In itself this statement indicates a lack of marketing orientation but bear in mind that marketing is about making profits as well as satisfying customers.

3.6 Segmentation is a process that should be used by both small and large companies. In fact, some smaller companies know their customer segments very well and manage to provide the right products for them. The corner shop where you buy your newspaper probably stocks only products which are needed by you and the people who live in the local vicinity. This is an excellent example of segmentation.

Benefits of effective segmentation

3.7 The segmentation process can be costly and time consuming. However, if it is done effectively it provides many advantages. Even the attempt to segment markets forces the marketer to become more aware of the unique needs of customer segments.

3.8 Because of the precise market definition, the marketer can create a specific marketing mix to meet the needs of his segment(s). He can focus market development, develop profitable pricing strategies, select appropriate channels of distribution and develop and target promotional messages. Remember, a business may decide to target more than one segment at a time, but the marketing mix may be adapted to suit each segment.

3.9 The marketer can follow the needs of his segment and can identify any change in needs so that he can respond quickly.

3.10 Because the marketer is attempting to satisfy a precise segment, he can efficiently allocate resources. All resources will be utilised so that satisfaction of his segment is achieved. This is often not possible in mass marketing.

3.11 The marketer will also benefit from the ability to identify his competition and will therefore be better able to analyse competitor strategy and behaviour. This may help to achieve a better competitive position for the marketer's products and brands.

3.12 Overall, effective segmentation provides benefits for both the marketing orientated company and its customers. Effective segmentation should result in greater sales and profitability and, because products can be 'finely tuned' to the needs of the market, greater customer satisfaction.

The target marketing process: three stages

3.13 We have talked generally about segmentation and we shall now look at a formal approach to target marketing as a whole. Figure 6.2 displays the target marketing process. It consists of three stages: market segmentation, market targeting and product positioning.

Figure 6.2 *Stages in market segmentation, targeting and positioning*

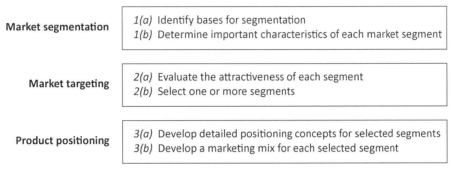

Adapted from Lancaster and Massingham (Essentials of Marketing)

3.14 **Stage 1** involves dividing the market into groups of customers who will require separate marketing mixes. Once a company has divided the market into groups or segments, it can develop a profile of customers within each segment. Many variables are used to segment markets and these are known as **segmentation bases**.

3.15 **Stage 2** of the process involves **the selection of suitable segments**. Many businesses choose to satisfy more than one segment at a time. According to Kotler, market segments must exhibit four characteristics if they are to be useful.

- **Measurability** – the degree to which the size and purchasing power of the segments can be measured. Certain segmentation variables are difficult to measure. An illustration would be the size of the segment of teenage smokers who smoke primarily to rebel against their parents. The marketer would find it difficult to get information about this market.
- **Substantiality** – the degree to which the segments are large and/or profitable enough. A segment should be the largest possible homogeneous group worth going after with a specific marketing programme.
- **Accessibility** – the degree to which the segments can be effectively reached and served. A vodka manufacturer might find that heavy users of its brand are men who go out late at night and frequent bars. Unless this group lives or shops at certain places and is exposed to certain media, they will be difficult to reach.
- **Actionability** – the degree to which effective programmes can be formulated for attracting and serving the segments. A small airline, for example, might identify seven market segments, but the number of staff in the company may be too small to develop separate marketing programmes for each segment.

3.16 **Stage 3** of the segmentation process is **product positioning**, which involves establishing effective marketing mixes to satisfy the segment(s) a business has chosen.

Chapter summary

- The marketing mix comprises the 4Ps of marketing: product, price, place and promotion. Marketers apply a balanced mix of all four elements when marketing a product or service.
- The service sector in developed economies has seen huge growth in recent decades.
- Services differ from tangible products in important ways. For this reason, marketers talk about the 7Ps of service marketing: product, price, place, promotion, people, process and physical evidence.
- In this context, 'process' means the policies, procedures and systems that support service delivery.
- The target marketing process can be broken down into three stages: market segmentation, market targeting, and product positioning.

Self-test questions

Numbers in brackets refer to paragraphs where you can check your answers.

1   List the four elements of the product marketing mix. (1.3)

2   List possible pricing strategies. (1.15)

3   List possible methods of product promotion. (1.24)

4   Suggest reasons for the growth in the services sector in developed economies. (2.2)

5   List characteristics that distinguish services from tangible products. (2.3)

6   What are the additional three elements in the extended marketing mix? (2.4)

7   List examples of 'physical evidence' in the marketing of services. (2.10)

8   Define market segmentation. (3.1)

9   What are the benefits of effective segmentation? (3.7ff)

10   What are the three stages of the target marketing process? (3.13)

CHAPTER 7

Competitive Advantage

Assessment criteria and indicative content

2.3 Explain sources of competitive advantage sought through marketing

- Sources of competitive advantage
- Competitor profiling and analysis

Section headings

1   The concept of added value
2   Competitor profiling and analysis

1   The concept of added value

Sources of competitive advantage

1.1 Professor Michael Porter argued that competitive advantage comes from the value a company creates for its customers. Value is the 'worth' of the product or service: what it costs the organisation to produce and what the customer is willing to pay for it. In other words:

- A firm creates value – by performing its activities better, differently or more efficiently than its competitors.
- Customers purchase value – measured by comparing a firm's products and services with those of its competitors.

1.2 The term 'added value' refers to a product acquiring greater value or worth as a result of all the processes that support it. Customer service is an obvious example, but it is possible to see the concept of adding value from a number of different perspectives.

Perspectives on added value

1.3 According to Porter, the ultimate value a firm creates is measured by the amount customers are willing to pay for its products or services above the cost to the firm of carrying out all its value-creating activities (production, service, logistics, marketing and so on). A firm is profitable if the realised value to customers (what they are prepared to pay) exceeds the collective cost of the firm's value-creating activities.

1.4 From an accounting perspective, therefore, added value is total revenue minus total costs of all activities undertaken to develop and market a product or service. This expresses the amount of economic value that has been added to the organisation's resources: how efficiently they are being used and how effectively they are being leveraged. From this perspective, you can add value either by inducing customers to pay more or by reducing costs. Seen from the customer's perspective, it means selling an equivalent product at lower prices (while maintaining viable profit margins), or providing additional product features or services to attract a premium price.

1.5 Value addition can be achieved through cost reduction or process efficiency. One of the most effective ways is to reduce the order cycle time by getting the goods to the market faster: this could be achieved by developing a well-managed and controlled supply chain that minimises waste and costs.

Porter's value chain model

1.6 The value chain is the sequence of business activities by which value is added to the products or services produced by an organisation or supply chain. It embraces the entire process from raw materials to finished delivered product and continuing after-sales service.

1.7 The value chain concept may be used to identify and understand specific potential sources of a firm's (or supply chain's) competitive advantage. The value chain separates out the strategically important activities of the business, in order to gain fuller understanding of the value of each.

1.8 Porter's value chain model shows total value as a combination of the value added by the activities of a business unit: Figure 7.1. (Note that these value adding activities are not the same as business functions: they may be carried out across departments.)

Figure 7.1 *Porter's value chain*

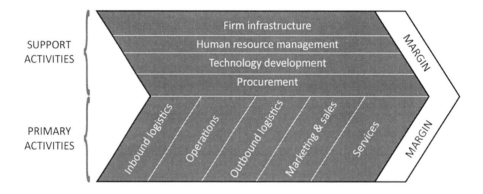

1.9 Primary value activities are grouped into five areas.

- Inbound logistics are the activities concerned with receiving, storing and disseminating inputs: materials handling, warehousing, inventory control etc.
- Operations are concerned with the transformation of inputs into finished goods or services. In manufacturing, these activities include assembly, testing, packing and equipment maintenance; in service industries, basic service provision.
- Outbound logistics are concerned with storing, distributing and delivering the finished goods to customers: warehousing, materials handling, transport planning, order processing and so on.
- Marketing and sales are responsible for communication with the customers to provide a means by which they can purchase the product (as well as an inducement to do so): market research, new product development, advertising and promotion, sales force management, channel management, pricing and so on.
- Service covers all of the activities which occur after the point of sale to enhance or maintain the value of the product for the customer: installation, repair, training, parts supply and maintenance.

1.10 The secondary, or support, activities operate across the primary activities, as in the case of procurement where at each stage items are acquired to aid the primary functions.

- Firm infrastructure refers to systems and assets for planning, finance, quality control and management.
- Human resources are all the activities involved in recruiting, deploying, retaining and developing people in the organisation.
- Technology development activities relate to both equipment, systems and methods of work organisation: product design and improvement of production processes and resource utilisation.
- Procurement is all activities to acquire inputs for primary activities.

The contribution of purchasing

1.11 Porter's value chain model relates to the entire organisation, and adopts primarily a manufacturing perspective. We need to focus now on the specific contribution that purchasing can bring, and to consider all organisations, including service firms and public sector bodies.

1.12 We commented earlier that value can be added either by cutting costs (but without loss of quality or product features), or by operational efficiency (leading to superior quality or product features at no additional cost). Ideally, we aim to achieve both of these objectives: improved output at reduced cost.

1.13 Here are some of the ways in which purchasing can help.

- By selecting appropriate suppliers they can improve the quality of inputs, with consequent improvement in the quality of outputs.
- By effective negotiation and/or tendering they can reduce the cost of inputs.
- By effective functional management they can reduce the cost of processing purchase transactions.
- By effective dialogue with user departments they can improve specifications so that purchasing needs are fulfilled more efficiently and at lower cost.
- By effective liaison with user departments and suppliers they can ensure that inputs surplus to requirements are eliminated.
- By effective inventory management they can minimise the costs of acquiring and holding stock.

1.14 To improve purchasing's efforts in this area we are concerned with measuring performance. In a newly developed purchasing function the initial emphasis may be on cost reduction, relating both to the cost of inputs and to the cost of running the purchasing function. (The focus is on improving **efficiency**.) In a more developed purchasing function, measures may be introduced for more strategic aspects of the role, such as supplier relationship management. (The focus is on improving **effectiveness**.)

1.15 Table 7.1 highlights some possible measures relating to both efficiency and effectiveness.

Table 7.1 *Efficiency and effectiveness of purchasing*

MEASURES OF PURCHASING EFFICIENCY	MEASURES OF PURCHASING EFFECTIVENESS
Basic purchase price of inputs	Quality of output
Cost of placing an order	Quality of service to customers
Cost of staffing the purchasing function	Achieving objectives within budget
Speed of transaction processing	Quality of supplier relationships
Use of information technology	Impact on profitability
Efficiency of organisational structure	Prompt delivery to customers
Efficiency of supplier management	

2 Competitor profiling and analysis

Who are our competitors?

2.1 Competition is the existence of rival products or services within the same market. Marketers must survey competitors thoroughly, including such critical strategic elements as their R&D capabilities, sales, services, costs, manufacturing and procurement.

2.2 The first problem is to establish who exactly is the competition. The question is simple to understand but sometimes difficult to answer. Competitors may not be producers of similar or directly competing products: for example, the competitors of a book publisher include publishers of other products, such as texts on CD-ROM and audio books, as well as publishers of videos and computer packages.

2.3 To identify competitors, marketers may need to check out any or all of the following possibilities.

- Obvious majors in the market
- The next best competitors, region by region
- New, big companies, with troubles of their own and possibly looking for new markets
- Small domestic companies perhaps operating in small premium market niches
- Foreign companies, with special emphasis on the first unobtrusive move into small domestic markets
- Oddball forays from unexpected competitors

2.4 In a market where several organisations are competing, marketing choices will depend partly on what a competitor is doing or is expected to do soon. A simple example would be a price reduction by a competitor which could lead to a price war if other suppliers follow suit. This is more likely to be important if the competitor concerned is one of the major players in the market, perhaps because of a large market share, or because of highly differentiated or focused products or services.

Competitor profiling

2.5 A detailed profile should be built up on each major competitor. Some competitors span many industries, whereas others are part of multinational organisations. Some are concerned almost exclusively with the domestic market, while others depend on exports for a high proportion of their sales.

2.6 Although it is tempting to evaluate a company's position solely on the basis of whether its products and services are superior to those offered by its competitors, there is a wide range of additional factors that determine competitive success. In fact, all the elements making up consumer preference, such as product quality, service, price and location are only part of the competitor analysis.

2.7   Another part of the process is to examine the internal strengths and weaknesses of each major competitor. In the long run, a company possessing strong operational assets, with an organisation structure and industrial culture conducive to motivation and innovation, and having ownership of significant financial resources, will prove to be a tough and enduring competitor.

2.8   A competitor profile should include coverage of goals, capabilities and performance.

- In terms of goals, we need to know the stated goals and the real priorities of our competitors. We also need to estimate their likely future goals and the changes they are likely to make in pursuit of them.
- In terms of capabilities, we need to know their core competencies and the resources they have to build upon. What are their particular competitive advantages?
- In terms of current performance we are interested in details such as managerial ability, operational performance, distribution channels, pricing strategy, financial strength and organisational structure.

Competitor analysis

2.9   There is of course an ethical element surrounding this area. Nobody is recommending that we 'spy' on competitors in any way that would be unethical, or even illegal (eg by issuing bogus requests for tenders). There are plenty of sources of information that do not require unethical or unprofessional behaviour to access them.

2.10   To begin with, we can often look at our competitors' products simply by observing them in retail outlets or by buying them. If it is a service we are interested in, we can inquire about the service or purchase it (perhaps in the guise of 'mystery shoppers') and then analyse how well the service was provided. We can also observe our competitors' promotional literature (point of sale information, advertisements, websites etc).

2.11   Other information published by competitors will include financial statements (usually annually, but more frequently in the case of listed companies). This can be supplemented by credit reference checks through organisations such as Dun & Bradstreet.

2.12   We can also keep an eye on job advertisements, which may give useful information on personnel policies and capabilities. General coverage of our competitors' activities in the national or trade press will also be useful. Specialised companies offer scanning and collation services: we can specify what we are interested in and the service provider will scan relevant press sources to provide us with relevant 'clippings'.

2.13   Networking is another important source of information. This will typically take place at trade exhibitions and conferences. We also need to network effectively with our own customers: they are probably hearing from our competitors and our sales personnel can glean important information from this source.

2.14   Finally, we may be able to gain information from our competitors' suppliers (especially if they supply to our own organisation as well – because we will then be in regular contact with them).

Chapter summary

- Porter argues that competitive advantage comes from the value a company creates for its customers.
- Porter's value chain model distinguishes between primary activities (inbound logistics, operations, outbound logistics, marketing and sales, and service) and support activities (firm infrastructure, human resource management, technology development, and procurement).
- Purchasing can contribute to added value both by cutting costs and by increasing efficiency.
- It is important to scan the market with a view to identifying and profiling competitors or potential competitors.
- There is an ethical issue in competitor analysis, but it is perfectly legitimate to gain as much information as possible by inspection of competitor products, review of competitors' accounts and so on.

Self-test questions

Numbers in brackets refer to paragraphs where you can check your answers.

1 What is meant by 'added value'? (1.2)

2 List the primary and support activities in Porter's value chain. (Figure 7.1)

3 How can purchasing contribute to added value? (1.13)

4 List some measures of purchasing efficiency and purchasing effectiveness. (Table 7.1)

5 List possible classes of competitors. (2.3)

6 What elements should be included in a competitor profile? (2.8)

7 Suggest sources of information for a competitor analysis. (2.10–2.14)

CHAPTER 8

The Relevance of Marketing to Purchasers

Assessment criteria and indicative content

2.4 Explain the relevance of marketing principles to purchasers

- Organisational buying behaviour
- Applying the 4Ps or 7Ps to the work of procurement and supply functions

Section headings

1. Organisational buying behaviour
2. Applying the marketing mix to procurement

1 Organisational buying behaviour

The buying centre concept

1.1 In the early 1970s Webster and Wind developed the 'buying centre' concept in order to structure large-scale sales in complex corporate environments. They identified five roles typically carried out in an organisational buying decision. In the early 1980s, Thomas Bonoma expanded their original list of five roles with the role of initiator. The concept then classified six buying roles for members of the organisation in the purchasing process.

1.2 In a company, a purchase depends on the person making the purchase decision as well as on the many employees who want to exert influence. A buying centre makes joint purchase decisions as an informal group. Its task consists of information acquisition, search processes, the development of choice criteria and decision making among alternatives.

1.3 The buying centre has three principal aspects.

- *Composition*: the size, hierarchical levels and functional areas involved
- *Influence*: those individuals with the most influence in the buying process
- *Roles*: the identification of different roles played by buying centre members

1.4 A buying centre includes all members of the purchasing organisation who play any of six roles in the purchase process.

- INITIATOR first identifies the need to buy a particular product or service to solve an organisational problem.
- INFLUENCER exerts influence on the buying centre's buyers and deciders.
- DECIDER ultimately approves all or any part of the entire buying decision – whether to buy, what to buy, how to buy, and where to buy.
- BUYER holds the formal authority to select the supplier and to arrange terms and conditions.

- USER consumes or uses the product or service.
- GATEKEEPER controls information or access, or both, to decision makers and influencers.

1.5   The Webster and Wind model structured organisational buying processes that are characterised by multi-person involvement levels, extensive internal and external coordination and long lead times. An individual can facilitate or assume more than one role in the purchase process and several individuals may hold the same role.

1.6   The concept of the buying centre is very useful as it can help in developing effective marketing strategies. It aids marketing in categorising those in a company that have a defined role in the buying process. That in turn will help marketing to target their approach in a way that is both effective and represents good value for spend. Understanding how marketers are targeting purchasers will aid you in making judgments about supplier offerings.

Influences on organisational buyer behaviour

1.7   As we saw in Chapter 1 there are internal and external factors that influence organisational behaviour. Internal influences are those within the organisation. The purchaser can influence and has a certain degree of control over these factors. External factors are outside the company's control.

1.8   Purchasing has a link role between companies as it is a point of contact between the buyer and the supplier. The role links internal factors with external factors.

Marketing from the supplier's perspective

1.9   Organisational buying is driven by derived demand, that is, demand for an end product or for a product or service sold by the buyer's customers. The demand for components by a manufacturer will be dependent on demand coming from their customers, the retailers and wholesalers, who in turn are reacting to demand from their customers, the consumers. Overall consumer demand may in turn be impacted by economic, social, political and technological factors in the environment.

1.10   Buying patterns for habitual purchases and frequent low-risk purchases, where little evaluation is required, follow similar processes as for individuals. These tend to use routine procurement practices such as inventory management, purchasing cards or buying via online catalogues.

1.11   Complex, large or infrequent purchasing decisions usually involve many more participants and are usually much more formal in process. Organisational purchase decisions are also capable of being of very large scale and can involve purchases for large amounts of money, take many months if not years to transact, and influence the careers of those involved.

1.12   These complex transactions are often in situations where the specification or the problem and/or the solution is difficult. In environments where problems are dynamic and interact with a developing and changing society and economy and where solutions evolve with knowledge and technology, the specifications themselves evolve. Often the buyer needs the active support of the supplier to understand the problem or to understand the state of possible solutions.

1.13   It may take the active support of the supplier to uncover the requirements, especially where the supplier has much greater knowledge of the problem environment. Thus, it is not unusual for a deep relationship to develop between buyer and supplier as the project evolves. Trust, integrity, empathy and openness often become key characteristics of the final decision process.

1.14 Many large organisational purchases involve consultative selling, that is where the buyer and vendor work together to define the problem, identify a solution and work together throughout a long process of implementation and support. Because of the relationship issues which occur in a long association, trust, integrity, empathy and engagement become important factors to consider in the buying decision.

1.15 A good proportion of organisational buying is controlled or constrained by the economic situation. Components, ingredients and supplies must fit with the conversion process and with the economic objectives of the final outcome. Some decisions are constrained by mandated decision rules which limit the scope of the decision making power of the actors, especially in public sector procurement.

1.16 Organisational buying is not entirely predictable or entirely rational. Individuals who specify requirements or provide technical input, those who search for information and others who undertake evaluations will still be influenced by their own past experiences, knowledge and training. If a rigorous process of information search and evaluation is not undertaken or if there is time pressure to make a decision, then not all vendors will be considered or fully evaluated.

1.17 In a complex one-off buying situation, an organisation will proceed through a series of steps to arrive at the buying process itself. Externally or internally some trigger kicks off the process. At this point, some part of the organisation defines the issues and seeks permission to do something about it. Some individual or department is then given responsibility to investigate and recommend action. A budget needs to be assigned and the process of establishing the need and investigating possible solutions commenced. This process can be complex where multiple organisational units are involved and where organisational change is involved.

1.18 The challenge for the supplier is clear. For the potential supplier the focus is primarily on the original 4 Ps of the marketing mix in order to gain the business, with increasing focus on the overall 7 Ps when securing the business. For the incumbent supplier the need is to be seen as the supplier of first choice. The marketing effort is targeted toward the service elements of the marketing mix.

2 Applying the marketing mix to procurement

2.1 In the previous section we looked at approaches that marketers would have in marketing their products and services to the decision making group and to purchasing in particular. Many purchasers do not feel they are the target of marketing. They fail to appreciate the time, effort and professionalism that suppliers put into winning their business and keeping it.

2.2 This might be because of the contrast between consumer marketing which surrounds us all the time and business-to-business marketing that tends to be more low-key, interpersonal and specific. Business-to-business marketing has developed at a rapid pace in recent years. Procurement in particular has undergone a rapid strategic change in organisations, raising its profile and position in the hierarchies of many companies.

2.3 Procurement manages the spend of the organisation. In consequence it is a natural target for the marketer with a host of marketing tools at their disposal.

Price

2.4 A supplier will have a defined approach to pricing that will consider how much money they intend to make from a product, how many they can sell at that price, and what market share they will get in relation to other suppliers. Suppliers tend to be very good at the price element of the marketing mix.

2.5 As a purchaser you will know how important research is when dealing with suppliers. The more you know about a company and the market it is operating in the better your judgment of the price. Getting competitive quotes sets something to benchmark against. However price is rarely or never the only consideration.

2.6 The reason we research the supplier is partly to understand their motivations in regard to price. Is the quotation fair and reasonable? If it is too good to be true we should ask why. Do they have a cashflow problem? Are they offering a low price as their factories are operating at less than full capacity? What will happen to our order when a more lucrative order comes in?

2.7 To understand price effectively we need to have a good understanding of cost structures used by suppliers and how the information gained from analysis can be used effectively in the sourcing, purchasing and negotiation processes. The ability to interpret a set of accounts and realise when suppliers are using definitions of 'profit' that suit their objectives is an important skill in purchasing.

2.8 In business markets price will often include after-sales service and support, guaranteed delivery of spares, additional warranties and many other additional factors. These can serve to mask the asking price. As a purchaser we need to place a value on these add-ons in order to work back and arrive at the true price. Getting three quotes, for example, is only useful for comparison purposes if we are comparing like with like.

Tips on price negotiation

2.9 Never accept the first offer – make a **low counteroffer** in return. The other party is likely to come back with a revised figure. Always ask what else they can include at the given price.

2.10 If the price is suspiciously low, ask yourself why. Are the goods of sufficiently high quality? Do they really offer value for money? What will after-sales service be like? You can also try to make the asking price look high by exposing any ongoing costs. Ask about repair costs, consumables and other expenses. If the current state of the supplier's market means prices are falling, point this out.

2.11 If the price includes features you don't need, try to lower it by asking to remove those features from the deal. Use your bargaining power to get a good deal. For example, if you're a big customer of the supplier, you could ask for **bulk discounts**. If you squeeze the price too low – perhaps by threatening to walk away from the negotiations – you may end up getting a poor deal. The supplier may have to cut costs elsewhere – in an area such as customer service, which could prove costly to you in the long run.

2.12 Even if you are a supplier's main customer and enjoy most of the bargaining power, forcing it to meet low prices at which it could go out of business will damage your reputation as a highly valued customer. The supplier will soon look for other customers and is likely to feel resentful.

With prices falling across many sectors, organisations are feeling the pressure. For many it means revisiting the pricing structure, analysing the overall package and looking at what customers are willing to pay.

2.13 The optimum price point is one where customers can meet their supply requirements at the lowest possible cost and suppliers can produce at optimum efficiency and maintain a profit. There is increasingly a split between suppliers with relatively high costs attached to their associated specialist services, and commodity suppliers, who can supply at a lower price point and maintain profit. The optimum price therefore is very different for these two areas.

2.14 Buyers naturally lean towards lower cost solutions and to a large extent have the power in determining market prices. With increasing numbers of products and services now available by catalogue, mail order and the internet, buyers are now often exposed to lower prices and wider choice and this is putting downward pressure on prices.

2.15 For the purchaser it is important to realise the impact of marketing on price. If you understand the supplier you are dealing with and their aims and objectives with regard to price you are in a better position when it comes to negotiation.,

Product

2.16 Marketing is about identifying, anticipating and satisfying customer needs. A marketer needs to be sure that his products and services meet and continue to meet customer needs.

2.17 Marketing research is the main tool that enables marketers to do this. Carrying out simple research can be accomplished by asking customers the following questions.

- What do they think of each product or service?
- How satisfied are they with the quality?
- How satisfied are they with any support services provided?
- How effective are the product, service and support in meeting their needs?

2.18 The purchaser, particularly if there is an existing relationship with a supplier, should assist in completing any questionnaires and by being honest in any meetings. It is only with accurate feedback that the supplier can improve their product or service offering in a manner that suits customers.

2.19 The marketer needs a system for collecting and analysing this feedback from customers in order that ideas can be fed into a new product development process that is ongoing. Marketers will look at where each product sits on the product lifecycle with the objectives of assessing the future of a particular product and adapting the marketing mix to suit the product at its particular stage in its lifecycle.

Promotion

2.20 The promotional mix is made up of five elements.

- Advertising
- Sales promotion
- Public relations
- Direct marketing
- Personal selling

2.21 The combination of these tools that a marketer uses depends on the budget that is available, the message he wishes to communicate and the target group of customers. In B2B markets advertising tends to be low-key and restricted to specialist journals, catalogues etc. The majority of advertising campaigns of the type we are familiar with are more focused towards consumer markets.

2.22 The use of sales promotion is not limited to consumer products marketing. In business-to-business markets sales promotions are also used as a means of moving customers to action. However, the promotional choices available to the business-to-business (B2B) marketer are not as extensive as those found in the consumer market.

2.23 For example, most B2B marketers do not use coupons as a vehicle for sales promotion with the exception of companies that sell to both consumer and business customers (eg products sold through office supply retailers). The techniques most likely to be used include price reductions, trade-in allowances, trade shows, internet catalogues and press releases.

2.24 For the marketer these methods need to be used selectively and in a manner that supports the product offering. In many business sectors trade shows are an established opportunity to get your company and your products seen.

2.25 Technology plays an increasing part in B2B marketing. In many ways development in business-to-consumer (B2C) marketing have been adapted to the B2B market. Internet sites are effective if well designed and easy to use. Often the purchaser will order product direct from the website using their company password and details. While there, the purchaser's attention could be drawn to a number of offers or deals that might prove attractive. By storing past information the suppliers website or catalogue can be programmed to flag up items that the purchaser has bought before or to offer similar alternatives.

Place

2.26 'Place', from a marketing perspective, is the means of distribution selected, depending on the type of product or service being offered. The choice of distribution channel is important as it will impact on pricing and promotion decisions in particular.

2.27 If we sell through wholesalers and retailers the marketer needs to consider that each will want their own mark-up, increasing the price to the final customer. We will also need to promote products and services to all members of the channel. Wholesalers and retailers will need to be persuaded to stock products and end customers to buy them. If we are selling to business we will have to cover the cost of a sales force. This can be an expensive option.

2.28 In purchasing many transactions, but not all, are direct with manufacturers. The consideration and perception of 'place' can be quite different. Place also covers the actual delivery of the goods and/or services.

2.29 When negotiating with a supplier one of the points negotiated will include delivery of the goods: delivery to one site or multiple sites, guaranteed delivery times, storage of the goods etc. All need to be considered and costed by the purchaser to ensure that the price and service quoted are appropriate. For international transactions the use of the appropriate incoterm, which provides a demarcation line where risk and responsibility pass together with allocation of responsibility for delivery to an agreed point or place, needs to be fully evaluated.

Chapter summary

- Organisational buying is more complex than consumer buying. In particular, the buying decision is made not by a single individual, but by a 'buying centre' or 'decision making unit'.
- Organisational buying is driven by derived demand: we buy supplies not for our own use, but with a view to incorporating them in the offering we make to our customers.
- Despite the greater formality involved in organisational buying, it is not an entirely predictable or rational process.
- Purchasers often fail to appreciate the effort and professionalism with which they are targeted by marketers. It is important that purchasers understand the principles and techniques of marketing.
- Price is invariably the element of the marketing mix that most concerns buyers. Expertise in price negotiation (and negotiation generally) is an important part of the buyer's toolkit.

Self-test questions

Numbers in brackets refer to paragraphs where you can check your answers.

1   Explain the 'buying centre' concept. (1.1, 1.2)

2   What are the six buying centre roles identified by Webster and Wind? (1.4)

3   What does it mean to say that organisational buying is driven by derived demand? (1.9)

4   How can a buyer determine whether a supplier's quoted price is 'fair'? (2.6)

5   List tips on price negotiation. (2.9ff)

6   What are the five elements of the promotional mix? (2.20)

8

CHAPTER 9

Profiling Purchasers and Suppliers

Assessment criteria and indicative content

3.1 Explain the main techniques for the profiling of purchasers and suppliers

- The application of the portfolio analysis matrix
- The application of the supplier perceptions and other matrices to procurement and supply

Section headings

1 The relationship spectrum
2 A portfolio of relationships
3 The supplier perceptions matrix
4 Appraising relationship success

1 The relationship spectrum

1.1 Commercial relationships may vary widely in the extent of their intensity, mutuality, trust and commitment – in other words, their 'closeness'. Writers often refer to a relationship 'spectrum' extending from one-off arm's length transactions at one end to long-term collaborative partnerships at the other: Figure 9.1.

Figure 9.1 *The relationship spectrum*

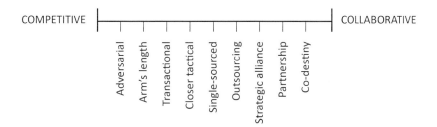

1.2 In Table 9.1 we highlight some of the main features of each relationship type.

Table 9.1 *The relationship spectrum explained*

RELATIONSHIP TYPE	CHARACTERISTICS
Adversarial relationship	Buyer and supplier are 'opponents', each striving to obtain advantages at the other's expense. There is little trust, communication or co-operation, and there may be open conflict (complaints, disputes and so on) in pursuit of advantage.
Arm's length relationship	A distant, impersonal relationship, where the buyer does not need close or frequent access to the buyer. Purchases are infrequent and of low volume, so investment in closer relationship is not justified.
Transactional relationship	Regular dealings may be established, but are still seen in terms of one-off transactions rather than relationship.
Closer tactical relationship	The buyer needs to secure quality and availability of supply, and therefore adds a degree of commitment (eg fixed or call-off contracts) and collaboration (eg on quality control) to the relationship.
Single-sourced relationship	In relation to a particular item or range of items, a buyer grants exclusivity to a single supplier. This implies a high level of trust, and requires mutual commitment and collaboration.
Outsourcing relationship	In order to focus on its core competencies, an organisation selects an external supplier to provide goods or services previously sourced in-house. An even higher level of trust, commitment and collaboration is required to ensure that standards are maintained.
Strategic alliance	Two (or more) organisations identify areas in which they can collaborate to deliver a joint offering. For example, a software developer might form an alliance with a training firm, the trainer providing accredited courses in using the software.
Partnership relationship	Buyer and supplier agree to collaborate closely for the long term, sharing information and ideas for development. There is a very high level of trust and the aim is to find solutions that benefit both parties, with gains and risks shared between them.
Co-destiny relationship	An even closer relationship, in which buyer and supplier link their businesses together strategically for long-term mutual benefit.

1.3 There are various versions of the spectrum model, some of which are surveyed in your recommended reading (Lysons & Farrington) – although they rely on concepts such as 'core competencies' and 'strategic alignment' which should be beyond the scope of this module (which focuses on operational relationships). Cox's 'stepladder of contractual relationships', for example, describes a spectrum including (in order of increasing closeness and mutual dependency):

- *Adversarial leverage*: multi-sourcing and hard-negotiated short-term contracts for routine purchases, where no unique competence is required of suppliers
- *Preferred suppliers*: smaller list of potential suppliers on the basis of vendor rating and accreditation, for more important purchases where some special competence is required of suppliers
- *Single sourcing*: purchasing strategic supplies from a single quality supplier who can offer distinctive, important competencies
- *Network sourcing and partnerships*: partnerships between the main buyer and a first-tier supplier, which develops partnerships with second-tier suppliers, to integrate and control the wider supply chain
- *Strategic supplier alliances or joint ventures*: formation of a jointly-owned separate firm to produce the supplied product or service, where the buyer and supplier's competencies are complementary and of equal importance.

1.4 Moore (in *Commercial Relationships*) offers a further version of the spectrum, which mixes type or closeness of relationship (as in our general model) with examples of purchasing approaches used (particularly at the transactional and arm's length end of the spectrum).

- **Spot buying**: making one-off purchases to meet requirements as they arise, taking advantage of best available terms at the time.
- **Regular trading**: giving repeat business to a group of preferred (known, trusted) suppliers.
- **Call-off contracts**, framework agreements or blanket ordering: establishing agreed terms of supply with suppliers for a defined period, against which individual orders can be made as required. (Effectively, an 'option to buy' from the supplier on agreed terms.)
- **Fixed contract**: establishing an agreed purchase volume or frequency, at agreed terms of supply, for a defined period.
- **Alliance**: agreement to work together with a supplier for mutual advantage in a particular area (eg a collaborative promotion, staff training or cost reduction)
- **Strategic alliance**: agreement to work together with a supplier for long-term mutual advantage in a particular area (eg systems integration or joint new product development)
- **Partnership**: agreement to work closely together for the long term, and on a range of issues, for collaborative problem-solving and development.

1.5 Lysons & Farrington argue (citing *Tang*) that the closeness of the buyer-supplier relationship – vendor, preferred supplier, exclusive supplier or partner – will influence (and be influenced by) operational factors such as: the type and length of the supply contract; the number of suppliers; the product or service provided; the amount and quality of information exchange; the pricing scheme and delivery schedule; the extent of senior management involvement; and the extent of supplier development and support offered by the buyer.

Adversarial or competitive relationships

1.6 In adversarial relationships, each party seeks to obtain the best possible outcome for itself, at the expense of the other party if necessary. This can be seen as a potential 'win-lose' situation, where any gains for the buyer are at the expense of the supplier, and *vice versa*. For example, the buyer gets the best price by squeezing the supplier's profit margins, or the supplier enhances its profit margins by cutting corners on quality.

1.7 Such relationships are characterised by:

- Lack of trust and therefore little information sharing
- A one-off or short-term transaction focus
- The use of power and negotiation to seek the best possible deal (even at the expense of the other party and the potential for ongoing relationship)
- Rigorously enforced compliance with contract terms (in the absence of shared responsibility for quality or improvements)
- Little co-operation or recognition of mutual interests.

1.8 These relationships are 'transactional' rather than 'relational'. There is no consideration of the effect of an adversarial approach or win-lose result on the potential for future dealings – since in any case, the buyer uses multiple other suppliers to stimulate competition. If the buyer alienates one supplier with its hard bargaining, there is always another one available.

9

Co-operative or collaborative relationships

1.9 With a transactional approach, the benefits of doing business together arise purely from exchange: money in return for goods or services. In a relational approach, the benefits of doing business together arise from sharing, collaboration and synergy (2 + 2 = 5).

1.10 In collaborative relationships, the parties intentionally seek to develop long-term, mutually beneficial ongoing dealings. The strategic view is that both buyer and supplier share common interests, and both can benefit from seeking ways to add value in the supply chain. 'Enlarging the pie' offers a win-win situation, where buyer, supplier and end-customer can all benefit.

1.11 The buyer seeks to develop long-term relationships with a smaller number of preferred suppliers. Relationship management is based on trust and mutual obligation, rather than mere compliance with contract terms. Both parties will participate in looking for improvements and innovations, secure in the knowledge that any benefits that are achieved will be shared. They will jointly set targets for improvements in cost and quality, and meet regularly to discuss progress towards achieving these targets. Information will be shared more or less freely (in areas of shared activity) in both directions, to support joint problem-solving and development.

1.12 Note that a collaborative relationship is a proactive relationship with the aim of securing improvements – not just a long-term cosy customer-supplier relationship where both parties have grown complacent and used to the *status quo*.

Partnership relationships

1.13 Partnership relationships are at the highly co-operative and committed end of the relationship spectrum. They are more 'strategic' (concerned with the long-term objectives of the organisation) and of longer duration. There is more trust and sharing of information. The supplier is seen as an integral part of the organisation's competitive advantage and future plans.

1.14 Partnering has been defined as: 'A commitment by both customers and suppliers, regardless of size, to a long-term relationship based on clear, mutually agreed objectives to strive for world class capability and effectiveness.'

1.15 The key characteristics of partnership sourcing are as follows.

- Top-level management commitment
- Involvement by all the relevant disciplines and functions
- Customer and supplier working together (eg there is likely to be early supplier involvement in new product design)
- A high level of trust, knowledge sharing and openness between customer and supplier, extending to the sharing of cost data by both parties (cost transparency)
- Clear joint objectives
- Commitment to a long-term relationship
- A proactive approach to improving and developing the partnership (rather than a reactive approach to dealing with problems after they have arisen)
- A **total quality management** philosophy, focused on co-operative efforts to maximise quality and secure continuous improvement
- Flexibility, as a result of enhanced trust and communication
- A high degree of systems integration (eg using EDI).

1.16 Lysons and Farrington note that: 'Partnering aims to transform short-term adversarial customer-supplier relationships focused on the use of purchasing power to secure lower prices and improved delivery into long-term co-operation based on mutual trust in which quality, innovation and shared values complement price competitiveness'.

2   A portfolio of relationships

2.1 From our discussion above, the temptation may be to think that a collaborative relationship would be 'best' or 'ideal' – or at least 'more enlightened' – even if, in practice, adversarial relationships are common. This is not necessarily the case, however, and you should be prepared to take a contingency view of the most appropriate relationship type for a given purchasing situation: in other words, 'it all depends'.

2.2 The most appropriate relationship type for a given purchasing situation may depend on factors such as the following.

- The nature and importance of the items being purchased: low-value, routine or one-off purchases are unlikely to justify heavy investment in long-term collaboration – whereas complex, customised, high-value purchases in unstable supply markets may well justify such investment, in order to secure control over the supply specification, quality and availability
- The competence, capability, co-operation and performance of the supplier (and reciprocal conduct of the buyer), and therefore the degree of trust developed between them: trust being a necessary foundation for closer relationship
- Geographical distance: close relationships may be more difficult to establish and maintain with overseas suppliers, especially if there is little communication infrastructure
- The compatibility of the supply partners: if their strategic aims, values and systems are incompatible, it may be too costly to attempt to bridge the distance or overcome the barriers (as long as more compatible alternatives are available)
- The organisation's and purchasing function's objectives and priorities: best available price, security and quality of supply and so on
- Supply market conditions: if supply is subject to risk (eg owing to weather or economic conditions), the buyer may wish to multi-source. If prices are fluctuating, it may wish to use opportunistic spot-buying – *or* to lock in advantageous prices through fixed contracts. If the market is fast-changing and innovative, it may avoid being locked into long-term supply agreements. If there are few quality, capable and high profile suppliers, it may wish to enter partnership with them – and so on
- Legal and regulatory requirements. Some types of relationships are regulated to protect competition (eg by forbidding cartels, collusion and mergers that would unfairly dominate a market and distort competition; or by ensuring compulsory competitive tendering in the public sector). As another example, in some developing economies, foreign suppliers are required to partner with local companies

When is a transactional approach appropriate?

2.3 A collaborative approach is not necessarily more suitable than a competitive approach to dealing with suppliers.

- A more adversarial approach may well secure the best commercial deal, and the biggest share of value from the relationship – where this is the priority.
- Developing collaborative relationships takes time and effort, and it is unrealistic to devote such resources to *all* relationships. They may not be possible for particular suppliers (eg

because the supplier isn't interested) or suitable (eg because the supplier is incompatible), and they may not be cost-effective for routine items (eg office stationery), or items which are only purchased rarely, so that collaboration would not add value in any significant way.

- There are risks in long-term relationships, for example: the risk of supplier complacency or opportunistic behaviour, based on the security of the relationship; the risk of being locked into relationship with the 'wrong' partners; the difficulties of measuring the effectiveness of co-operation in meaningful ways; problems in obtaining an equitable sharing of the risks and rewards of co-operation (if the coalition is dominated by one more powerful party).

Drivers of collaborative relationships

2.4 However, a number of drivers have contributed to the trend towards more collaborative supply chain relationships.

- Perception of strategy has widened to embrace competitive advantage from supply chain management. Whole supply chains – not just individual firms – compete with each other in the global marketplace.
- Product lifecycles have shortened: that is, they come into and out of 'fashion' more quickly. This has created the need for faster product development, more frequent product 'updating', and responsive product customisation (eg Dell's customer-specified computer packages) – all of which put pressure on supply chain communication and collaboration.
- Organisations are increasingly outsourcing non-core activities to external contractors, enabling them to concentrate on core activities where they have distinctive competencies and where most value can be added. This creates a need for close relationship, so that the firm can minimise risk by retaining some control over output quality and other potentially reputation-damaging issues (such as environmental and ethical performance).
- ICT developments have, enabled and supported inter-organisational networking and relationships.
- In economies increasingly dominated by service-based and knowledge-based sectors, and consumer branding, there is pressure for companies to protect and leverage their intellectual property, knowledge, relationship networks and brand values: this depends on close, trusting co-operation within the supply network.
- In an increasingly challenging business environment, a focus on arms' length, opportunistic transactions fails to leverage the competitive and value-adding potential in supply chain relationships: eg opportunities to gather customer feedback; or to collaborate on product improvement or cost reduction; or to share knowledge and best practice with other companies to improve the performance of the industry as a whole.
- There are costs of adversarial relationships. They tend to encourage compliant (rather than committed) performance, disputes, win-lose negotiation and opportunistic behaviour, loss of preferential treatment that might arise from goodwill and trust, loss of potential synergy and improvements (eg from information-sharing) and so on.
- With competitive pressures towards 'lean' supply, closer relationships and integration help to reduce waste in supply chains. Partners can work together to identify wastes such as unnecessary or duplicated activity, bottlenecks, delays, errors and rejects, and excess inventory – and opportunities for improvements. Closer relationships often also result in integration of information systems, which streamlines transaction processes.
- 'Best practice' supply techniques, such as total quality management and just in time supply, reduce tolerance for delays and errors in the supply process. This causes increased dependence on the supply chain, which in turn requires strong supplier relationships, and the closer integration of people, plans and systems, both internally and externally.

- From the supplier's point of view, there has been a major shift towards relationship marketing (especially in business-to-business markets), mainly because it is more profitable to retain and develop existing customer relationships than to acquire new customers.

2.5 There are certain contexts in which partnership sourcing, in particular, may be most beneficial.

- Where the customer has a high spend with the supplier
- Where the customer faces high risk: continual supply of the product or service is vital to the buyer's operations, regardless of its market value
- Where the product supplied is technically complex, calling for advanced technical knowledge by the supplier (and making the cost of switching suppliers high)
- Where the product is vital and complex, requiring a lot of time, effort and resources ('high hassle') to manage
- Where the supply market for the product is fast-changing, so that an up-to-date knowledge of technological or legislative changes in the market is essential
- In a restricted supply market, where there are few competent and reliable supplier firms – and closer relationships could therefore improve the security of supply.

2.6 The advantages and disadvantages of collaborative or partnership relationships, from both the buyer's and the supplier's perspective, are summarised in Table 9.2.

Table 9.2 *Advantages and disadvantages of partnering*

ADVANTAGES FOR THE BUYER	DISADVANTAGES FOR THE BUYER
Greater stability of supply and supply prices	Risk of complacency re cost and quality
Sharing of risk and investment	Less flexibility to change suppliers at need
Better supplier motivation and responsiveness, arising from mutual commitment and reciprocity	Possible risk to confidentiality, intellectual property (eg if suppliers also supply competitors)
Cost savings from reduced supplier base, collaborative cost reduction	May be locked into relationship with an incompatible or inflexible supplier
Access to supplier's technology and expertise	Restricted in EU public sector procurement directives (eg re-tendering after 3–5 years)
Joint planning and information sharing, supporting capacity planning and efficiency	May be locked into relationship, despite supply market changes and opportunities
Ability to plan long-term improvements	Costs of relationship management
More attention to relationship management: eg access to an account manager	Mutual dependency may create loss of flexibility and control
ADVANTAGES FOR THE SUPPLIER	DISADVANTAGES FOR THE SUPPLIER
Greater stability and volume of business, enabling investment in business development	May be locked into relationship with an incompatible or inflexible customer
Working with customers, enabling improved service, learning and development	Gains and risks may not be fairly shared in the partnership (depending on power balance)
Joint planning and information sharing, supporting capacity planning and efficiency	Risk of customer exploiting transparency (eg on costings, to force prices down)
Sharing of risk and investment	Investment in relationship management
Cost savings from efficiency, collaborative cost reduction, payment on time	Dependency on customer may create loss of flexibility and control
Access to customer's technology and expertise	Restricted by EU public sector procurement directives
More attention to relationship management: eg access to a vendor manager	May be locked into relationship, despite market changes and opportunities

9

A portfolio of relationships

2.7 In the end, an organisation may need to develop a *portfolio* of relationships, appropriate to each supply situation.

- Using the Pareto principle or 80: 20 rule, the organisation might focus its relationship investment on the 20% of suppliers who provide 80% of total supply value – or the 20% of customers who provide 80% of total sales revenue. It might also prioritise suppliers and customers according to other measures of importance – as we will see below – and develop closer relationships with more important players.
- The organisation may use a blend of approaches. An 'adversarial-collaborative' approach, for example, might allow it to work co-operatively with a supplier on product development, cost reduction or continuous improvements – *and* to negotiate hard in order to secure the best possible share of the resulting value gains. In other words, collaboration 'enlarges the pie' – of which competition seeks to gain a bigger slice.

2.8 A writer called Ralf (cited by Lamming and Cox) sums up the situation.

'The good old-fashioned Rottweiler approach to buying must co-exist with a more collaborative approach internally and externally... Adversarial relationships exist, and rightfully so. What is needed, however, is a balance between both approaches and a sophisticated understanding of which tactic to use to develop the strategic goals of the organisation. Deciding which relationship is necessary and when is crucial. If this is not done, then companies can be sucked into relationships they do not want, and that often generate higher costs, or time consuming activities and behaviour that are dysfunctional.'

2.9 So how do you 'decide which relationship is necessary and when'? One tool that can help is the purchasing portfolio matrix developed by Peter Kraljic.

Kraljic's purchasing portfolio or relationship matrix

2.10 Kraljic drew up a matrix to classify purchases according to two dimensions: supply risk (including factors such as sourcing difficulty, and buyer vulnerability to supply or supplier failure) and purchase value (including factors such as the profit potential of the item, and the importance of the purchase to the business). The matrix therefore has four quadrants, as follows: Figure 9.2.

Figure 9.2 *The Kraljic purchasing portfolio matrix*

Complexity of the supply market

	Low		High	
High	**Procurement focus** Leverage items	**Time horizon** Varied, typically 12-24 months	**Procurement focus** Strategic items	**Time horizon** Up to 10 years; governed by long-term strategic impact (risk and contract mix)
	Key performance criteria Cost/price and materials flow management	**Items purchased** Mix of commodities and specified materials	**Key performance criteria** Long-term availability	**Items purchased** Scarce and/or high-value materials
	Typical sources Multiple suppliers, chiefly local	**Supply** Abundant	**Typical sources** Established global suppliers	**Supply** Natural scarcity
Importance of the item	**Procurement focus** Non-critical items	**Time horizon** Limited: normally 12 months or less	**Procurement focus** Bottleneck items	**Time horizon** Variable, depending on availability vs short-term flexibility trade-offs
	Key performance criteria Functional efficiency	**Items purchased** Commodities, some specified materials	**Key performance criteria** Cost management and reliable short-term sourcing	**Items purchased** Mainly specified materials
Low	**Typical sources** Established local suppliers	**Supply** Abundant	**Typical sources** Global, predominantly new suppliers with new technology	**Supply** Production-based scarcity

2.11 At a strategic level, the Kraljic matrix is used to examine an organisation's purchasing portfolio and its exposure to risk from supply disruption. For the purposes of this syllabus, it can be seen more simply as a tool for assessing what types of supplier relationships are most appropriate for different types of purchases.

- For *non-critical or routine items* (such as common stationery supplies), the focus will be on reducing transaction costs. Arm's length approaches such as blanket ordering (empowering end users to make call-off orders) and e-procurement solutions (eg online ordering or the use of purchasing cards) will provide routine efficiency.

- For *bottleneck items* (such as proprietary spare parts or specialised consultancy services, which could cause operational delays if unavailable), the buyer's priority will be to ensure control over the continuity and security of supply. This may suggest approaches such as negotiating medium-term or long-term contracts with suppliers; developing alternative or 'back-up' sources of supply; and including incentives and penalties in contracts to ensure the reliability of delivery.

- For *leverage items* (such as local produce bought by a major supermarket), the buyer's priority will be to use its dominance to secure best prices and terms, on a transactional basis. This may mean taking advantage of competitive pricing; standardising specifications to make supplier switching easier; and using competitive bidding and/or buying consortia to secure the best deals.

- For *strategic items* (such as key subassemblies bought by a car manufacturer, or Intel processors bought by laptop manufacturers), there is likely to be mutual dependency and investment, and the focus will be on the total cost, security and competitiveness of

9

supply. There will therefore be a need to develop long-term, mutually beneficial strategic relationships and relationship management disciplines (eg cross-functional teams, vendor management, account management and so on).

3 The supplier perceptions matrix

3.1 The Kraljic model illustrates the buyer's perspective: how important and desirable are supplier relationships for a given purchase? However, in this module it is equally important to see the other side of supply chain relationships. A buyer may want to enter into a relationship with a supplier – but how does the supplier feel about the buyer as a prospective long-term client? (And given that the focal firm will also be a supplier to its own customers, how does it decide whether to seek long-term relationships with them?)

3.2 The supplier preferencing model is another matrix, this time illustrating how attractive it is to a supplier to deal with a buyer, and the monetary value of the buyer's business to the supplier: Figure 9.3.

Figure 9.3 *The supplier preferencing model*

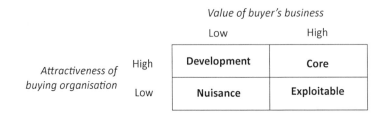

3.3 Looking at each quadrant in turn:

- Nuisance customers are neither attractive nor valuable to do business with. Suppliers practising customer relationship management will regularly review their customer base and downgrade or cease service to unprofitable customers – or raise their prices (in such a way as to turn them into exploitable customers).
- Exploitable customers offer large volumes of business, which compensates for lack of attractiveness. The supplier will fulfil the terms of the supply contract – but will not go out of its way to provide extras (and any extras demanded will be charged at additional cost).
- Development customers are attractive, despite currently low levels of business. The supplier may see potential to grow the account, and may court extra business by 'going the extra mile' in fulfilling contracts: if all goes well, the customer may be converted to 'core' status.
- Core customers are highly desirable and valuable for suppliers, who will want to establish long-term, mutually-profitable relationships with them if possible.

3.4 This is a useful model for operational supplier relationship management, because it suggests strongly that in order to get the best from suppliers, a buyer needs to maintain its 'attractive customer' status. There are various factors that might make a supplier keen to do business with a buying organisation, and therefore (potentially) more co-operative, flexible and committed.

- Glamorous or high profile brand: suppliers will want to deal with the organisation in order to enhance their own reputation and attractiveness to customers
- Good reputation and standing in the market eg for environmental or ethical leadership
- Fair, ethical and professional trading practices (eg paying suppliers promptly, not entering into unnecessary disputes, keeping suppliers well informed, not squeezing supplier profit margins

excessively)

- Willingness to collaborate and co-invest in capability and performance improvements (eg through supplier training and other forms of supplier development, information-sharing for collaborative cost reduction and continuous improvement programmes etc)
- Willingness to share risks, costs and value gains equitably with supply partners (ie seeking reciprocity or win-win: not making excessive demands and hard bargaining techniques, without offering any benefits or concessions in return)
- Constructive interpersonal relationships with contacts at the buying firm (although these are vulnerable to change, if contacts leave the firm).

4   Appraising relationship success

Introduction

4.1   Purchasing must assess whether and how far its relationship with a supplier is satisfactory, in order to provide feedback for learning and adjustment. This may partly be done by supplier appraisal, on the basis that if the supplier is underperforming, there must be something wrong with the buyer-supplier relationship, or how it is being managed. However, aspects of the buyer-supplier relationship *itself* may be part of purchasing's own performance appraisal.

4.2   Evaluation will be concerned with key aspects of the supply relationship, including:

- Whether the relationship is being suitably managed, given its priority, importance and potential to add value
- Adherence to contract terms (in relation to volume, quality, on-time delivery, service levels, payment terms, dispute resolution and so on)
- Operational efficiency, in terms of scheduling (and changes to schedules), specifications, communication and information-sharing and so on
- The quality of rapport, communication and problem-solving built up between contacts in the two organisations
- The stage of trust reached in the relationship
- The fair sharing of the risks, costs and rewards of doing business together
- How effectively, positively and collaboratively problems and disputes are resolved
- The willingness and potential for the relationship to develop further and to offer added value or competitive advantage for the supply chain.

Relationship mapping

4.3   Relationship mapping is a way of analysing, classifying and prioritising relationships: that is, deciding which relationships are most valuable and profitable for the organisation, and therefore worth concentrating investment of time and money in.

4.4   The best known form of relationship map in a purchasing context is **Kraljic's relationship matrix** (or **purchasing portfolio matrix**). This may be used to evaluate whether the organisation's relationship with a supplier is of the right type to 'fit' the profile of the type of goods being purchased, and whether resources are being efficiently deployed across the purchasing portfolio, to maximise relationship leverage.

4.5   The **supplier preferencing matrix** (sometimes referred to as the 'supplier perceptions' matrix) can be used to prioritise and evaluate relationships with (internal and external) customers: which customers are valuable and worthy of investment, and which can be exploited or terminated? It can also be used to assess the purchaser's own status as a customer to its suppliers: is it an attractive and valuable customer, or does it risk being exploited or terminated? Can it increase its attractiveness (by being more congenial to deal with, or offering benefits to suppliers) or can it increase its volume or value of business (eg by consolidating orders)?

4.6 Both of these models were discussed above.

Purchaser-supplier satisfaction

4.7 Leenders, Fearon, Flynn & Johnson (*Purchasing and Supply Management*) point out that the assessment of a buyer-supplier relationship is not always clear cut. Different parties may have different perceptions of its effectiveness. In addition, while in simple transactions the buyer's assessment may depend on immediate rapport with the supplier's sales representative, in the case of a long-term partnership relationship, the assessment will be based on past and current performance *and* personal relationships *and* future expectations. And such assessments may change over time.

4.8 Leenders *et al* provide a framework for clarifying a current purchaser-supplier relationship. Supplier and purchaser each score the relationship from 1 to 10, according to how satisfied they are with it: Figure 9.4.

Figure 9.4 *A purchaser-supplier satisfaction model*

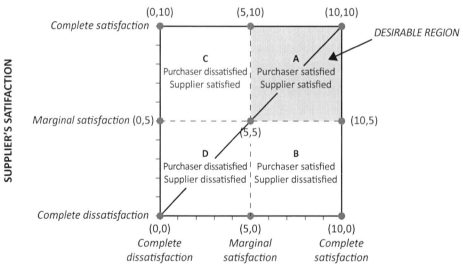

4.9 Looking at each quadrant of this model:

- In the bottom left quadrant, nobody is satisfied. Both parties will want to change the relationship – or to leave it.
- In the bottom right quadrant, the buyer is at least marginally satisfied, but the supplier is not – and in the top left quadrant, the positions are reversed. In either case, the dissatisfied party will be seeking to change or leave the relationship.
- In the top right (desirable) quadrant, both parties are relatively satisfied, although there may be room for improvement to reach the ideal situation of (10, 10), where both parties are perfectly satisfied with the relationship.

4.10   The diagonal line in the diagram is the line of 'stability' or 'fairness'. Movements up or down this line indicate equal improvement (or deterioration) for both parties. The further up the line the relationship is rated, the greater its overall stability (commitment, loyalty and likelihood of continuance), because there is less pressure for change from one party or the other.

4.11   Mapping a given supplier-customer relationship onto this grid gives both parties a starting point for improvement planning. It focuses attention on relationships which are least satisfactory, or most unstable (creating supply risk), and therefore have the most need of improvement and the most potential to improve. In addition, it may act as a starting point for dialogue about *why* one or both parties is dissatisfied, and what can be done to improve matters.

Chapter summary

- There is a spectrum of possible buyer-supplier relationships, ranging from competitive to collaborative.
- Despite the modern trend towards collaborative relationships, there is still a place for old-fashioned adversarial relationships.
- An important task for purchasing is to identify the appropriate relationship for each supplier. This will depend on many factors, but above all on how critical the particular procurement is.
- Kraljic's matrix is a well established tool for selecting appropriate supply relationships. It attempts to classify purchases in terms of (a) their supply risk and (b) their financial importance.
- The supplier perceptions matrix indicates how suppliers value their customers, in terms of the customer's inherent attractiveness and the volume of business on offer.
- It is important for both buyers and suppliers to evaluate supply relationships. One possible model for doing so is the 'satisfaction model' developed by Leenders et al.

 ## Self-test questions

Numbers in brackets refer to paragraphs where you can check your answers.

1   List possible supply relationships from left to right along the relationship spectrum. (1.1)

2   List possible approaches to purchases from spot buying to partnership. (1.4)

3   Define partnership relationships. (1.14)

4   List key characteristics of partnership sourcing. (1.15)

5   What factors may influence our choice of buyer-supplier relationship? (2.2)

6   What factors have driven the modern trend towards collaborative relationships? (2.4)

7   List advantages and disadvantages of partnering from the buyer's perspective. (Table 9.2)

8   Sketch the Kraljic matrix. (Figure 9.2)

9   Sketch the supplier perceptions matrix. (Figure 9.3)

10   List key aspects of a supply relationship that should be evaluated. (4.2)

CHAPTER 10

Information Exchange in the Supply Chain

Assessment criteria and indicative content

3.2 Classify the types of information that can be exchanged between purchasers and suppliers

- Types of information exchange such as scheduling difficulties, demand forecasts, trends in costs and availability, designs and innovations and new product development

Section headings

1 Supply chain information flows
2 Environmental information
3 Key stakeholder information
4 Data gathering tools and techniques

1 Supply chain information flows

1.1 Information is a key resource for organisations. Nothing can be done or decided without it.

1.2 Information flows and exchanges take place at all levels of the organisation. Martin Christopher *(The Strategy of Distribution Management)* illustrates the information requirements within a supply chain management system, and the types of information most commonly used at different levels in the organisation hierarchy: Figure 10.1.

Figure 10.1 *Hierarchy of use for the purchasing information system*

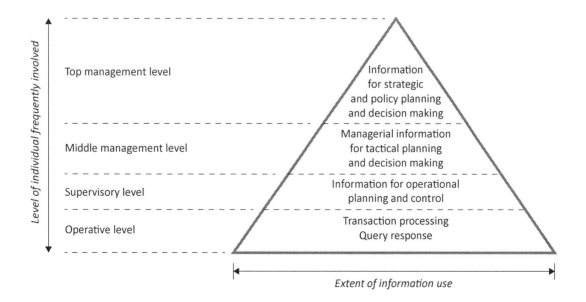

Level of individual frequently involved

- Top management level — Information for strategic and policy planning and decision making
- Middle management level — Managerial information for tactical planning and decision making
- Supervisory level — Information for operational planning and control
- Operative level — Transaction processing / Query response

Extent of information use

1.3 This syllabus focuses on operational relationships, so let's start there.

Types of information required for purchasing activities

1.4 The **purchasing cycle** is a model which breaks the basic purchasing process down into its component stages. Purchasing procedures vary widely from one organisation to another, and according to the nature of the transaction, but there are certain stages which a purchasing transaction will typically progress through. There are various versions of the cycle, classifying the stages differently. Table 10.1 sets out some of the commonly identified stages of the cycle and examples of their information requirements.

Other types of information required across supply chains

1.5 In addition, information is used across supply chains for the following purposes.

- To determine strategic resource requirements (eg through demand forecasting)
- To anticipate customer needs and wants (eg through market research) and to develop new products and services (eg by consultation and ideas sharing between marketers, designers, engineers, purchasing and suppliers)
- To support innovation (eg by gathering information about what others are doing, monitoring technology development, sharing best practice)
- To support strategic planning and policy development (eg through environmental analysis, market research and purchasing research)
- To support risk management: gathering data on potential financial, competitive, supply and other risks, so that measures can be taken to minimise the likelihood of risk events occurring (eg by contingency planning and safeguards) – or to minimise the severity of the impact when they do occur (eg by taking out insurance)
- To support performance measurement and control (eg through results monitoring or stakeholder feedback, and comparison with plans, targets and standards)
- To support cost management (analysis of what it costs organisations to carry out their activities and source their resource requirements, and how costs can be managed or reduced) and pricing (what prices organisations need to charge their customers in order to attract customers and make a profit). This is an area in which information is sensitive – yet transparency may help buyers and suppliers to strike a mutually profitable balance, and to collaborate on supply-chain cost reduction.
- In stakeholder management (eg through stakeholder communication, education, consultation and feedback-gathering)
- In customer-supplier relationship management and development (eg through increasing information-sharing and contacts to build trust; increasing integration and co-ordination; performance monitoring and joint improvement planning; negotiation; and so on).

Stakeholder information requirements

1.6 Each of the stakeholders and participants in the supply chain will require information to fulfil its own objectives and perform its own activities. We will discuss some of these requirements, in relation to customers (internal, intermediary and consumer) and suppliers, in following sections of this chapter.

1.7 However, exam questions in this area may focus on specific stakeholders in specific industry or business contexts. You need to be able to transfer your general knowledge of information

Table 10.1 *The purchasing cycle and associated information requirements*

STAGE	DESCRIPTION	INFORMATION REQUIREMENTS
Need recognition	Identification and notification of a need or problem requiring purchasing of goods or services	Analysis of new product materials or components Forecasts of customer demand Rate of usage of materials and consumables Purchase requisition or bill of materials
Need definition	Systematic description of goods or services required: design, performance, technical and quality standards	Information on potential suppliers Information on technical requirements Quality, cost, schedule parameters
Evaluate sources	Investigation of the supply market, make/do or buy decisions and supplier appraisal	Supply market intelligence Costs and capabilities for 'make/do' option Supplier information (offerings, prices, capabilities, potential compatibility etc) Information for invitation to tender
Supplier selection	Selecting the preferred supplier of the goods or services	Order-winning criteria Supplier, product or service, availability data Tender or offer information from suppliers Information to support negotiations
Contracting	Awarding and developing a contract – or preparing and issuing a purchase order	Authorisation of decision Standard and negotiated contract or trading terms Legal advice for contract development Exchange of contract and order details
Contract management	Following up of the order, processing discrepancies and rejections, and checking that the terms of the transaction or contract have been met.	Progress monitoring, checking, reporting Comparison of performance v order or contract Feedback for problem-solving and adjustment Sign-offs, confirmations and receipts Contacts or exchanges for relationship management
Utilisation	Efficient deployment and utilisation of the goods or services once delivered	Monitoring and feedback on performance Notice of maintenance or service needs Inventory management data (stock levels and locations; lead times; customer demand, sales and usage data)
Payment	Payment for goods or services (may be on receipt, on completion, at stages through contract etc)	Review of transaction completion Authorisations and notifications to pay Invoices and payment requests from suppliers Invoice matching (to order, goods received) Funds transfer (eg via BACS, cheque) Payment receipts or reports and statements
Disposal	Decommissioning, recycling or disposal of items or waste products (where relevant)	Maintenance and performance information Accounting for depreciation Info re safety and green disposal issues
Performance review and learning	Reviewing the transaction or contract for future improvements and purchasing plans	Criteria and feedback re supplier and purchasing performance; process efficiency and effectiveness Potential to develop and improve the relationship Further need or replacement need: back to Stage 1!

10

requirements to specific cases. Use our categories and examples as a framework, adding contextualised detail appropriate to a given stakeholder. What form might transactional, planning, risk management or performance measurement data take in the case of an advertising agency, or a transport or logistics provider, or a retailer?

Purchasing information systems

1.8 An 'information system' consists of all the processes and technologies used to capture, store, retrieve, process and analyse, use and share information. Nowadays, the term generally refers to electronic (rather than paper-based) systems, but theoretically, a card index file is as much part of an information system as a computer is. The system may include hardware, software, people, communication systems and the data itself. Various forms of information system are used in organisations.

1.9 **Operational information systems** support the storage and handling of information required for the day-to-day activities of different functions. A purchasing information system would therefore include data on suppliers, purchases and prices – and tools for budgetary control, sourcing (eg tendering, requests for quotation), processing purchase transactions, gathering EPOS data for inventory management, expediting orders, handling invoices and so on.

1.10 **Database and database management systems** capture and store data (eg on customers, products, inventory, suppliers or transactions-in-progress) in a structured way, so that they can be shared by different users, and interrogated flexibly for a variety of applications.

1.11 **Decision support systems** are designed to assist middle managers in making and implementing tactical decisions about the best use of organisational resources. They use spreadsheets and computer models such as JIT, manufacturing resource planning (MRPII), or computer-aided design and manufacturing (CAD-CAM), to examine the effect of different inputs and scenarios on the outcomes of a plan or decision, to help managers evaluate and select the best options.

1.12 **Management information systems (MIS)** are more integrated systems to support strategic-level planning. They draw on information captured by operational systems (eg sales, purchase, point-of-sale, inventory, maintenance, HR, financial and business intelligence data), to generate reports and analyses for planning and control: results data, information analysis (forecasts, business scenario models, trend analysis) and so on.

1.13 Baily, Farmer, Jessop & Jones (*Purchasing Principles and Management*) describe the historical development of purchasing and supply chain management in terms of information systems development and – perhaps more importantly – integration.

- **Infant stage:** a simple manual clerical system, supporting operational decision-making and transaction processing within the purchasing department alone
- **Awakening stage:** improvement of the manual system, and exploration of computer processing, in response to the recognition of the importance of information to support purchasing decisions
- **Developing stage:** beginning to link purchasing IT systems with those of other functions, to support more integrated resource planning and management (eg materials requirements planning or MRP)
- **Mature stage:** full computerisation of purchasing information processing within the firm, with an integrated purchasing database supporting co-ordinated materials planning and

management (eg manufacturing resources planning or MRPII)

- **Advanced stage:** direct EDI link of internal purchasing database to the external supply chain (key customers and suppliers), for full integration of supply processes, efficiency of paperless transaction processing and enhancement of supply chain collaboration.

Databases

1.14 A database is a centralised collection of structured data, organised in such a way that:

- All relevant information is held within the system, and can be regularly monitored and amended to maintain its integrity, accuracy and up-to-dateness
- Different users are able to access and interrogate it according to their specific information needs.

1.15 The same data can be used for many different applications. Supplier details, for example, will be relevant to technical staff (to support purchase requisitions), purchasing staff (for generating orders), accounts personnel (for checking invoices against agreed terms) and so on. A buyer might be interested in the prices charged for a particular stock item by various suppliers, and will want to access all invoices which include that item; an account manager may want to inspect the history of dealings with a particular intermediary customer (because of credit control problems, say), and will want to access all invoices which include that customer.

1.16 An internal supply database may include a range of data about:

- Suppliers: products, materials and services available, prices, terms and conditions, quotations and contracts, delivery and quality performance (based on historical transactions), plant and management, contact details and so on
- Market variables: availability of materials, prices, trends (periodic shortages, price fluctuations)
- Inventory: stocks, usage rates, locations, value, standard re-order quantities
- Transactions: orders in progress, historical orders.

1.17 Databases can also be interrogated and the data analysed (using a process called 'data mining') for applications such as:

- Identifying the best suppliers (for purchase decisions) or customers (for targeted marketing effort)
- Developing the supplier or customer base (by identifying potentially valuable contacts and relationships to pursue)
- Enhancing supplier and customer relationships, by using information to personalise, target and streamline communications.

1.18 Databases ensure continuity of knowledge, service and relationships. People move on, and have limited memory capacity at best: databases allow historical and current data about supplier performance, customer preferences and inventory levels to be stored and retrieved as needed. However, an organisation need not rely only on its own knowledge base: databases compiled by other firms, institutions, research and consultancy services and other bodies can be accessed, by engaging their services – and/or often, nowadays, via the internet, on a free or subscription basis.

1.19 A typical information-based exam question might ask what information you would gather and store in a database of suppliers (or intermediaries, customers, competitors or supply market), and where you would find the information. We will now look at some of these issues.

10

2 Environmental information

Environmental intelligence

2.1 In this context, the term 'environment' does not refer to 'green' or ecological issues. We are referring instead to the external 'environment' of an organisation, which includes:

- The organisation's immediate operating (or 'micro') environment, incorporating customers, intermediaries, suppliers and competitors who directly impact on its plans and operations
- The general (or 'macro') environment, incorporating wider factors in the society in which the organisation operates (political, economic, social, technological factors and so on).

2.2 The external environment exerts an important influence on the organisation, in three basic ways.

- It presents *threats* (such as restrictive legislation, competitor initiatives, technology obsolescence or industrial action by trade unions, say) and *opportunities* (such as growth in market demand, technological improvements or more skilled workers entering the labour pool). These affect the organisation's ability to compete in its market and fulfil its objectives. Environmental threats and opportunities are key factors in the formation of business strategies and plans.
- It is the source of *resources* needed by the organisation (labour, materials and supplies, plant and machinery, energy, finance, information and so on). Environmental factors determine to what extent these resources are, or are not, available in the right quantity, at the right time and at the right price.
- It contains *stakeholders* who may seek, or have the right, to influence the activities of the organisation. An organisation must comply with laws and regulations, for example, in order to avoid legal and financial penalties, but it may also have to negotiate with employees, suppliers and customers – or bow to public opinion which might jeopardise its market or reputation.

2.3 Most organisations would carry out some kind of audit of environmental factors, opportunities and threats, as a preparation for making or changing strategic plans. Most large organisations also carry out some form of ongoing environmental monitoring or scanning. This involves continually gathering and analysing intelligence from sources such as trade journals and their websites; conferences and exhibitions; published reports and online databases (such as Mintel); published statistical sources and so on.

2.4 The organisation may also retain specialist consultants or advisers who have knowledge, experience and contacts relevant to a particular aspect of the environment – such as technology, law or social trends – or who specialise in the discipline of environmental analysis and risk management. However, one of the key roles of *any* manager (as identified by Henry Mintzberg) is that of 'Monitor': scanning the environment for information about changes, trends, threats and opportunities. This is one of the reasons for networking within your profession (other people are a great source of information), as well as reading quality newspapers and professional journals, and searching the internet with your eyes open.

PESTLE analysis

2.5 A popular tool for analysing the macro environment is described by the acronym PEST (and more comprehensive variants such as PESTLE), which sets out the main categories of environmental factors which impact on organisations. You may have come across this model in your previous studies. In any case, it is well worth remembering the categories: if you are asked in the exam to comment on 'external factors' or 'environmental factors', they provide a good checklist around which to build a well-structured answer.

2.6 A broad example of the kind of analysis that can be conducted, to support planning and decision-making, is shown in Table 10.2. Obviously, more specific factors or changes would raise more specific questions.

Table 10.2 *PESTLE analysis*

FACTOR	DESCRIPTION	ANALYSIS
Political	Government influence on your industry	What are the likely implications of a change in government policy?
Economic	Growth trends; patterns of employment, income, interest rates, exchange rates, tax rates etc.	How might changes affect future demand for your products or services, or future supply and cost of resources and labour?
Socio-cultural	Changing composition, attitudes, values, consumption patterns and education of the population	How might changes affect the demands and expectations of customers, suppliers and other stakeholders, or skill availability?
Technological	Changing tools for design and manufacturing, information and communications etc.	Are there opportunities for development – or risks of obsolescence? Are competitors adapting more quickly?
Legal	Law and regulation on business, employment, information etc.	How will the organisation need to adapt its policies and practices in order to comply with forthcoming measures?
Environmental/ ethical	Resources, sustainability, pollution management, weather, 'green' pressures	Which factors may cause supply or logistical problems, compliance issues, market pressure or risk to reputation?

Purchasing research

2.7 Purchasing research is 'the systematic study of all relevant factors which may affect the acquisition of goods and services, for the purpose of securing current and future requirements in such a way that the competitive position of the company is enhanced' (van Weele).

2.8 This is obviously a broad remit. It may include various forms of information gathering and analysis, including the following.

- Environmental audits, environmental (PESTLE) factor analysis and Strengths, Weaknesses, Opportunities and Threats (SWOT) analysis
- Industry analysis (the structure of the industry, its key players, and the nature and intensity of competition in the industry), competitor analysis (the actions, strengths and weaknesses of key competitors), and critical success factor analysis (what objectives must be achieved in order to secure competitive advantage)
- Supply, demand and capacity forecasting (eg using statistical analysis or expert opinion gathering) to estimate future sourcing requirements
- Vendor analysis: evaluating the performance of current suppliers, and potential suppliers not currently being used
- Market analysis: appraising general supply conditions in the market. What is the likely availability of each material, and are any shortages possible or probable? What is the prevailing price of each material, and what fluctuations (if any) are likely?

10

2.9 This research is conducted, on an ongoing or project basis, with the aim of providing information on the basis of which the organisation can plan to adapt to changes in the supply environment (ideally, earlier and better than its competitors) – to take advantage of new opportunities and/or to take defensive action in the light of perceived threats.

3 Key stakeholder information

3.1 In this section, we will draw together a broad checklist of some of the information requirements relating to customers and suppliers, as the key stakeholders in the supply chain. For each category of stakeholder, we will look at:

- Information required *by* the focal organisation *about* the stakeholder, in order to manage the relationship and supply chain processes. (Another way of looking at this is: what information would the organisation wish to gather for its supplier or customer database?)
- Sources of information about the stakeholder, from which the organisation may gather information for a supplier or customer information system
- Information required *by* the stakeholder *from* the focal organisation, in order to fulfil its role in the supply chain.

Information for locating potential suppliers

3.2 Information gathering will be required in order to locate potential suppliers in the supply market. A number of sources of information are available for this purpose.

- Information websites, which include business directories and listings, searchable databases designed to promote exports and specialist purchasing resources (such as the Purchasing Research Service)
- Online market exchanges, auction sites and supplier/buyer forums
- Published trade and industry directories and journals (which may carry news and feature articles, advertising, listings, statistical digests and so on)
- Trade and industry exhibitions and conferences (which may provide opportunities to view competing products, meet supplier representatives and gather literature)
- Trade associations (and their websites)
- The marketing communications of supplier organisations: brochures, catalogues, sales representatives, corporate website and so on
- Informal networking and information exchange (eg recommendations and referrals from other buyers).

Information in a supplier database

3.3 Once an organisation has an established supply base, it will usually store information about existing, past and potential suppliers in a supplier database. Information which could prove useful in supplier relationship management and developing supplier relationships is listed in Table 10.3.

Table 10.3 *Supplier information*

INFORMATION ABOUT SUPPLIERS	SOURCES OF INFORMATION ABOUT SUPPLIERS
Contact details (including details of account managers, where relevant)	Trade registers and directories, trade and industry exhibitions and conferences
Products and services offered	Supplier literature, websites, corporate reports and accounts
Standard or negotiated terms and conditions of trade, including prices, rates and fees where known (or record of prices previously paid or agreed)	Supplier sales and customer service staff
Approved, preferred, sole status of supplier	Feedback from own staff, vendor managers etc
Average value and frequency of spend with each existing supplier (used to identify key accounts)	Contract and transaction files and records
Special capabilities (eg plant, late customisation capability, EDI) suggesting supplier selection when special needs arise, or potential for future development	Reported financial and operational results (eg cost reductions, new product development, lead times)
Results of supplier appraisals, audits and ratings	Supplier appraisal, audit and rating reports
Vendor performance history: quality, lead times, delivery, compliance, disputes	Testimonials or reports from other customers (eg by request or business networking)
Comments on compatibility, commitment, innovation and other more subjective issues	Electronic performance monitoring (eg goods inwards tracking)
Current systems, framework agreements and call-off contracts in place	
Transaction histories, and transactions in process: orders outstanding, enquiries, the person dealing with the account etc (for contract management, order chasing, payment scheduling)	
Prices charged for stock items by various suppliers	

Supplier information requirements

3.4   Thinking through the purchasing cycle and supply chain information flows from the point of view of the supplier, some of the main types of information suppliers will require from a buying organisation in the course of business are listed below.

- Detailed, clear and accurate specifications of the product, service and service levels (ie a clear statement of the customer's expectations)
- Clearly stated expectations in relation to schedules, special needs, shared responsibilities, reporting and other matters relevant to fulfilling the contract – plus buyer values and policies about 'green' supply, CSR and other issues
- Standard terms and conditions of the buyer
- Accurate forecasts of levels of demand for the product or service (to support production planning) – and early warning of any change in forecast demand
- Feedback on performance (ideally in time to deal with problems before they become disputes)
- And so on.

3.5   In addition, suppliers will seek to compile a customer database. Since this will have the same requirements as a customer database compiled by the focal organisation on *its* customers, we will cover them under the heading of 'information about customers'.

10

Information in a customer/client database

3.6 Information which could prove useful in developing (external) customer relationships is listed in Table 10.4.

Table 10.4 *Customer information*

INFORMATION ABOUT CUSTOMERS	SOURCES OF INFORMATION ABOUT CUSTOMERS
Contact details (including details of vendor managers, where relevant)	Market research into customer needs, wants and preferences
Types of products and services purchased (to customise offers for cross-selling and up-selling) and any special requirements or preferences	Published market research reports and statistics
Standard or negotiated terms and conditions of trade	Corporate customers' literature, websites, corporate reports and accounts, tender info
Average value and frequency of spend (to identify key accounts) and/or available budget allocated	Reported results (eg sales patterns, sales by outlet or region, revenue growth or decline)
Estimated lifetime value: total value of business projected over potential duration of relationship	Account, transaction and enquiry records, giving historical purchase, complaint and enquiry data
Current or other suppliers, where relevant (ie direct competitors for contracts)	Capturing and developing customer contacts at exhibitions and conferences, sales visits
Media preferences and responses to promotions (eg 'where did you hear about us?') – to fine-tune marketing plans	Electronic data capture (eg Electronic Point of Sale data or website traffic monitoring)
Contact and transaction history: orders outstanding, payment history, enquiries, account managers on both sides etc.	Recommendations and referrals by other satisfied customers
Demographic information (in consumer markets): sex, age, occupation, location, interests – to define market segments, customise offers, personalise communications	Details provided by customers through website forums, extranet registrations, survey questionnaires, feedback forms, promotional competitions, informal info-gathering by customer service staff and so on

Information about intermediary customers

3.7 Additional information may be useful if the customer or client is a supply chain partner such as a retailer or distributor, in order to monitor its suitability, stability and performance in getting the product out to the market. For example:

- The turnover and profitability of the firm, and other indicators of its financial stability and creditworthiness (ie likely continuing demand for stock, and ability to pay for it)
- Sales of the supplying company's product(s), year on year, by region or sales outlet and/or by customer group, in order to measure the distributor's and products' performance
- Business terms, including discount levels, sale-or-return terms, requirements for contribution to marketing and display costs, arrangements for return of redundant stock
- Reputation and image of the firm, including any incidents which enhance (eg retail award) or damage (eg product recalls) its standing in the market
- Marketing and promotional methods, plans and spend, in order to monitor the effectiveness of advertising, sales promotions, in-store displays and so on – and to explore opportunities for joint promotions, perhaps
- Factors in the firm's competitive and external environment (PESTLE factors) which might affect its stability or effectiveness. (Examples may include commercial property rents,

business cycles, support for 'green' retail brands, competition from internet sales, trends towards out-of-town shopping centre locations and so on.)

Customer information requirements

3.8 Customers will primarily want to know exactly what is being offered in the total 'bundle of benefits' represented by a product, service or supply relationship: features, performance attributes, quality standards, service elements, price (and life-time costs of ownership), availability, delivery times and so on. Again, this will be the mirror image of 'information about suppliers', covered in Table 10.4 above.

Internal customer/client information

3.9 The purchasing function will require the same kind of information about internal customers' wants and requirements, and feedback as to their satisfaction with the service they receive. Likewise, it will have to offer the same kind of information about its services and the benefits of using them, and planning and work-in-progress data to facilitate co-ordination and control.

4 Data gathering tools and techniques

Qualitative versus quantitative data

4.1 Data can be divided into two basic types.

- **Quantitative** data is numerical or statistical data. Quantitative research answers questions such as: how many? What percentage or proportion? How often? How many times? How long? How much? Where?
- **Qualitative** data is subjective, diagnostic and pertaining to qualities or attributes that cannot readily be quantified: how well people do things, or why, or how satisfied or committed they are. It 'probes' rather than 'counts'.

4.2 Supply chain information systems require *both* sorts of information. It will interest a supplier to know how many of his products are being purchased, how frequently, and for how much; what proportion of transactions result in customer complaints or product returns; and (in consumer markets) what percentage of men aged 18–35, say, use similar products: this is quantitative data. However, it will also interest the supplier to know how customers go about choosing this type of product, what is important to them about it, what would make them change suppliers, and how satisfied they are with the supplier's performance: this is qualitative data.

4.3 Similarly, a buyer may want to collect quantitative data on a supplier's performance in terms such as cost, lead times, productivity (quantity of outputs in a given time), or other statistics such as the proportion of deliveries made on-time-in-full. But he may also want to consider qualitative issues such as the supplier's flexibility or commitment to quality, or the professionalism of customer service staff, or whether there is cultural compatibility between the two organisations.

4.4 Generally, techniques for gathering quantitative data involve various forms of counting or measurement. They include: observation; testing or experimentation; statistical survey questionnaires; the extracting of data from statistical or numerical records and reports (including purchase, sales and accounting records); and electronic monitoring (eg computerised recording of sales, inventory movements, purchase values, transport mileage and so on).

4.5 Generally, techniques for gathering qualitative data involve getting respondents (the subjects of the research question, or a representative sample of a larger target population) to express their views. They include: individual depth interviews and their group equivalent (focus groups), and various feedback mechanisms such as suggestion schemes, attitude surveys, feedback forms and complaint procedures.

Primary and secondary data

4.6 Another way of classifying data is to look at its sources.

- Primary data consists of original information (whether qualitative or quantitative), gathered to solve a specific research problem or question. In other words, the organisation goes out and finds its own data, or uses a research agency to do so on its behalf: this is sometimes also called 'field research'.
- Secondary data is information that has already been collected (by primary research) for some other purpose, made available to a wider user audience by publication. The organisation merely has to access the data: this is sometimes also called 'desk research'.

4.7 Secondary research is often less costly and time-consuming than primary research, because the data has already been collected and prepared for use. It is therefore generally used first: the information may answer the question without the need for primary research, or may help to ascertain what data remains to be gathered by primary research. However, if the organisation or procurement function wants to know what its suppliers or customers think about its performance, or proposed changes, it may need to conduct primary research.

Sources of secondary data

4.8 **Internal** secondary sources include information available to the researcher from his own company records: there is a wealth of such information available, although it may not be helpfully organised – and is often under-utilised. The purchasing function may have access to data from its own information systems, and those of other functions (eg technical, marketing, HR and financial data). Internal secondary sources include purchase and sale records, accounts, customer complaint records, invoice and inventory records, and so on. Such information allows us to measure past performance, trace the effect of actions on results, and perhaps even detect emerging trends and extend them into future forecasts.

4.9 There are also huge amounts of **external** secondary information, generated by other organisations including the government; research agencies and consultancies; publishers of directories, newspapers, periodicals, research reports; and compilers of databases. Sources include:

- Published financial reports and accounts
- Published statistical reports
- Specific industry or trade directories
- Newspapers and specialist trade, industry or purchasing journals (and their online equivalents)
- Trade and industry bodies and business networking
- Libraries, universities, embassies and consulates, chambers of commerce and other relevant information providers
- The internet – which may give access to any of the above listed sources.

4.10 Secondary data is often easy to gather, but this does not mean that it is quality information. It is always worth remembering that secondary information: may be inaccurate, biased or outdated (check the credibility of the source); may not be directly relevant to your needs; and may be equally accessible to your competitors (and so unlikely to lead, by itself, to any great competitive advantage).

Primary data-gathering

4.11 Four basic techniques are used to obtain primary data: observation, experimentation or testing, depth interviewing and surveys.

4.12 **Observation** means watching and observing people and processes in action. In market research, for example, consumers might be observed as they shop, or as they respond to point-of-sale displays and promotions. In supplier appraisal, a site visit may be used to allow the appraisal team to watch production, inspection or despatch processes. In internal performance improvement programmes, customer service or purchasing staff may be observed interacting with stakeholders (or telephone calls may be 'monitored for quality purposes').

4.13 Observation gives an objective picture of behaviour, which is often a more reliable guide than what people say they do or intend to do. However, it is labour-intensive, costly and time-consuming, and while it gives quantitative information on *what* is done, it does not necessarily give qualitative information on *why*.

4.14 **Experimentation** or testing involves trying out an action or change on a small scale, carefully observing and measuring the results and impacts on stakeholders. In market research, for example, consumers may be asked to sample or trial products and give feedback, or responses to advertising may be pre-tested for a test group or region. In purchasing, trial supply contracts may be used to test new supplier performance, or new procedures or systems may be trialled with a single supplier or product, prior to roll-out. Again, this is potentially costly and oriented more towards quantitative data.

4.15 **Depth interviews** involve asking target respondents (or representatives of the target group) for their opinions and responses on an issue. The interviews are usually quite unstructured, with a list of subjects for discussion, rather than specific questions to which answers will be obtained. This allows valuable qualitative information to emerge. Interviews may be one-to-one (eg with a senior member of a key customer, supplier or other stakeholder) or using representative groups of 5–25 people, called **focus groups**.

4.16 In market research, focus groups are often used to generate ideas for new product concepts, to explore consumer response to promotional and packaging ideas, and to gauge customer response to changes. Purchasing might use similar interviews to gauge supplier and internal customer attitudes to proposed supply chain changes (eg introducing e-procurement or outsourcing or off-shoring supply) or to generate new product development ideas. Depth interviews are expensive, and depend on the skill of the facilitator or interviewer and whether or not the respondents are truly representative and expressive. However, they are an excellent source of qualitative information. Focus groups, in particular:

- Encourage ideas generation, as participants' ideas are bounced off each other
- Demonstrate the way people form, express and change their opinions and responses in group settings and under the influence of opinion leaders and challengers (mirroring the way they will be tested in the market)

10

- Encourage unstructured expression, giving good qualitative information
- Allow for interactive question and answer, for the clarification and probing of responses where required.

4.17 **Survey research** is based on collecting data from answers to questionnaires. You have probably completed several questionnaires either in your working or home life, so you will have some awareness of the technique. It is often used in market research (customer surveys) and internal stakeholder management (employee attitude surveys). In a purchasing context, you might think of supplier, customer or internal client feedback forms, or supplier appraisal questionnaires.

4.18 Survey questionnaires can be issued by post or posted online, or conducted one-to-one over the telephone or in a face-to-face interview.

- Postal and online surveys are the most cost-efficient tool, since they are self-administered by the respondent. However, this does put pressure on the organisation or research agency to design a *good* questionnaire which is clear and easy to complete. It also limits the amount of information that can be gathered, and tends to be more effective at asking specific, factual questions – which elicit mainly quantitative information.
- Telephone and personal surveys allow an interviewer to guide and motivate the respondent in answering, and are better for asking 'open' questions, allowing respondents to express themselves more freely, and therefore eliciting qualitative information. (How do you feel about...? Why do you...?) They also tend to have a better response rate: while respondents can refuse to take part, they are less likely to do so than postal survey targets (who can simply ignore the questionnaire).

Chapter summary

- Different types of information are used at different levels within an organisation, and also at different stages of the purchasing cycle.
- Information systems are increasingly important in the activities of purchasing personnel. Baily et al identify a number of distinct stages in the development of purchasing information systems.
- An organisation's external environment presents threats, supplies resources, and contains stakeholders who may influence the organisation.
- A popular tool for analysing the external environment is PESTLE analysis.
- Organisations must engage in active information gathering as regards both their suppliers and their customers.
- Quantitative data is numerical or statistical. Qualitative data is subjective, and relates to attributes that cannot readily be quantified.
- Primary data is original data gathered to solve a specific research problem. Secondary data has been gathered originally for some purpose other than the one to which we are now applying it.
- Techniques of primary data gathering include observation, experimentation, depth interviews and surveys.

Self-test questions

Numbers in brackets refer to paragraphs where you can check your answers.

1   List information requirements arising at different stages in the purchasing cycle. (1.4)

2   What are the different types of information system required in purchasing? (1.9ff)

3   What is a database? (1.14)

4   In what three ways does the external environment impact on an organisation? (2.2)

5   What does PESTLE stand for? (Table 10.2)

6   List sources of information helping purchasers to locate potential suppliers. (3.2)

7   Distinguish between quantitative data and qualitative data. (4.1)

8   Distinguish between primary data and secondary data. (4.6)

9   Name four techniques for obtaining primary data. (4.11)

10 What are the main advantages of using focus groups? (4.16)

CHAPTER 11

The Impact of Technology

Assessment criteria and indicative content

3.3 Explain how technologies may impact on a commercial relationship between purchasers and suppliers

- Explanation of supplier and customer networks
- The applications of the intranet and internet in commercial relationships
- The use of electronic catalogues
- The use of technology to exchange data

Section headings

1. Supplier and customer networks
2. Internet and intranet
3. Electronic catalogues
4. The use of technology to exchange data

1 Supplier and customer networks

1.1 A supply chain is a network of retailers, distributors, transporters, storage facilities, and suppliers that participate in the production, delivery, and sale of a product to the consumer. The supply chain is typically made up of multiple companies who coordinate activities to set themselves apart from the competition.

1.2 A supply chain has three key parts.

- Supply focuses on the raw materials supplied to manufacturing, including how, when, and from what location.
- Manufacturing focuses on converting these raw materials into finished products.
- Distribution focuses on ensuring these products reach the consumers through an organised network of distributors, warehouses, and retailers.

1.3 A supply chain strategy defines how the supply chain should operate in order to compete in the market. The strategy evaluates the benefits and costs relating to the operation. Supply chain strategy focuses on the actual operations of the organisation and the supply chain that will be used to meet a specific goal.

1.4 Supply chain management is the management of a network of all business processes and activities involving procurement of raw materials, manufacturing and distribution management through to finished goods.

Supply chain management strategy

1.5   Supply chain strategies are the critical backbone to many business organisations. Effective market coverage and the availability of products at key locations depends upon the effectiveness of supply chain strategy. When a product is introduced in the market and advertised the need is to have the product where the customer is able to buy and take delivery. Any problem in product not being available at the right time can result in a fall in customer interest and demand which may be difficult to recover from.

Supply chain design

1.6   Designing a supply chain network for each industry or business involves arriving at a satisfactory design framework taking all elements into account. These will include product, market, process, technology, costs, and external environment. The design will include evaluating alternative scenarios suited to specific business requirements. No two supply chain designs can be the same.

1.7   The design of a supply chain network involves finding answers to the following questions.

- Procurement: Where are our suppliers? How will we procure raw materials and components?
- Manufacturing: Where will we locate the factories for manufacturing and assembly?
- Finished goods: Where will we hold inventories? What number and location of warehouses?
- Distribution: How will we distribute to markets?
- Information technology: How can we design a system that links the supply chain partners together?

1.8   A supply chain network structure is a series of strategic alliances formed to produce and market a product. These structures will bring the resources of the supply chain companies together on a long-term basis enabling reduced costs, quicker reaction times and enhanced quality not only in terms of the product but also in terms of the overall level of service.

1.9   Supply chains will be different in that they all have different beginnings (raw materials) and different endings (the customer) but all work in fundamentally the same way. The supply chain network links together all the actors, resources and activities both physically, through the movement of goods, and technologically, through the movement of information.

Information technology

1.10   Computer applications today manage multiple functions in supply chains. While applications primarily function as store houses of information, they also drive and enable processes in the supply chain. Various technology platforms collaborate and function to enhance supply chain network functions today.

1.11   Applications such as enterprise resource planning or ERP (with various modules covering all functions such as materials management, and supply chain management and many more core business enterprise systems) drive business processes in supply chain networks

1.12   These systems alone do not suffice. Many more applications to support these systems are used, depending on specific needs of the business. Supporting software may be used as standalone applications or integrated with the ERP. Most often it is found that the systems are used as standalone applications without having to integrate with ERP because of the cost of integrating and the effort involved.

1.13 In a highly evolved technology driven supply chain, it is essential to manage processes, events and deviations on a 24/7 basis. Multi process network, sharing knowledge, information, and enabling transactions can be managed only with an electronically enabled technology. These technology enterprises need to be able to work in collaborative mode and be supported by infrastructure and an IT strategy at the business enterprise level.

1.14 E-commerce has further redefined the way business is carried on. Online purchase has impacted the way supply chains are organised and markets are driven. Customer behaviour and preferences are changing as online marketing is establishing a one-to-one contact with the customer and is able to offer a personalised experience.

1.15 The instant delivery of the information through the internet elicits immediate response and action from the customer. The sales lead time is rapidly decreasing. The demanding customer therefore needs to be serviced immediately at the same speed.

1.16 Internet technology has further opened up geographical boundaries. Anyone, sitting in any corner of the globe, is able to purchase a product online at the click of a button. The companies have to be well equipped with the logistics and supply chain network to be able to service the customer.

2   Internet and intranet

The internet

2.1 The internet is a global system of interconnected computer networks that use the standard internet protocol suite to serve billions of users worldwide.

2.2 The internet is a *network of networks* that consists of millions of private, public, academic, business, and government networks, of local to global scope, that are linked by a broad array of electronic, wireless and optical networking technologies. The internet carries an extensive range of information resources and services, such as the inter-linked hypertext documents of the world wide web and the infrastructure to support email.

2.3 Most traditional communications media including telephone, music, film, and television are reshaped or redefined by the internet, giving birth to new services such as Voice over Internet Protocol (VoIP) and Internet Protocol Television (IPTV). Newspaper, book and other print publishing media are adapting to website technology, or are reshaped into blogging and web feeds. The internet has enabled or accelerated new forms of human interactions through instant messaging, internet forums, and social networking. Online shopping has grown rapidly and business-to-business and financial services on the internet affect supply chains across entire industries.

Intranets

2.4 An intranet is a private internal business network that enables companies to share information, to collaborate, and to improve their communications. In essence, an intranet is a business's own private website. It is a confidential business network that uses the same underlying structure and network protocols as the internet and is protected from unauthorised users by a firewall.

2.5 Intranets enhance existing communication between employees and provide a common knowledge base and storage area for everyone in the company. They also provide users with easy access to company data, systems and email from their desktops as long as they are authorised to access these areas. A personal login and password will allow access to certain areas but deny entry to others. For example, someone may have access to the marketing area but not the human resources area.

2.6 As intranets are secure and easily accessible via the internet, they enable staff to do work from any location simply by using a web browser. This can help business to be flexible and control office overheads by allowing employees to work from almost any location, including their home or customer sites.

2.7 Other types of intranet are available that merge the regular features of intranets with those often found in software such as Microsoft Office. These are known as online offices or web offices. Creating a web office allows us to organise and manage information and share documents and calendars using a familiar web browser function, which is accessible from anywhere in the world.

2.8 Here are some examples of content found on intranets.

- Administrative – calendars, emergency procedures, meeting room bookings, procedure manuals and membership of internal committees and groups
- Corporate – business plans, client and customer lists, document templates, branding guidelines, mission statements, press coverage and staff newsletters
- Financial – annual reports and organisational performance
- IT – virus alerts, tips on dealing with problems with hardware, software and networks, policies on corporate use of email and internet access, and a list of online training courses and support
- Marketing – competitive intelligence with links to competitor websites, corporate brochures, latest marketing initiatives, press releases, presentations
- Human resources – appraisal procedures and schedules, employee policies, expenses forms and annual leave requests, staff discount schemes, new vacancies
- Project management – current project details, team contact information, project management information, project documents, time and expense reporting
- External information resources – route planning and mapping sites, industry organisations, research sites and search engines

Benefits of an intranet

2.9 An intranet is a very effective internal communication tool within a business. Corporate information can be stored centrally and accessed at any time.

2.10 A virtual community can be created to facilitate information sharing, collaborative working and the sharing of resources and best practice. Better access to accurate and consistent information by staff members leads to enhanced levels of customer service. Paperwork is reduced as forms can be accessed and completed on the desktop, and then forwarded as appropriate for approval, without ever having to be printed out, and with the benefit of an audit trail.

2.11 Business efficiency can be improved by using an intranet for the following purposes.

- Publishing – delivering information and business news as directories and web documents
- Document management – viewing, printing and working collaboratively on office documents such as spreadsheets
- Training – accessing and delivering various types of e-learning to the user's desktop

- Workflow – automating a range of administrative processes
- Front-end to corporate systems – providing a common interface to corporate databases and business information systems
- Email – integrating intranet content with email services so that information can be distributed effectively

2.12 It is considered good practice to give the intranet a different image and structure from the customer-facing website. This will help to give internal communications their own identity and prevent employees confusing internal and external information.

Extranets

2.13 An extranet enables a business to communicate and collaborate more effectively with selected business partners, suppliers and customers. An extranet can play an important role in enhancing business relationships and improving supply chain management.

2.14 An extranet is similar to an intranet but it is made accessible to selected external partners such as business partners, suppliers, key customers and so on. It is used for exchanging data and applications and sharing information. As with an intranet, an extranet can also provide remote access to corporate systems for staff who spend a lot of time out of the office, for instance those in sales or customer support, or home workers.

2.15 Extranet users should be a well-defined group and access must be protected by rigorous identification routines and security features.

2.16 Businesses of all sizes are under increasing pressure to use online ordering, electronic order tracking and inventory management. At the same time small businesses are keen to meet the demands of larger companies in terms of working flexibly, adopting new technologies and enabling the exchange of business information and transactions.

2.17 Extranets offer a cheap and efficient way for businesses to connect with their trading partners. It also means that business partners and suppliers can access the information they need 24 hours a day. The ability of the extranet to automate trading tasks between trading partners can lead to enhanced business relationships and help to integrate a business firmly within its supply chain.

2.18 **Availability** and **security** are key factors in the success of an extranet. Significant resources, particularly in training and software, may be required to keep the content of the extranet accurate and up to date.

The internet and its impact on supply chain relationships

2.19 The internet enhances supply chain performance and can be considered crucial to e-commerce success. As the supply chain evolves in the information age, the internet's capability to support tight coordination between business and channel partners means that all the information, transactions, and decisions that are the essence of synchronised supply chains will flow through the web. Using the internet to connect the systems of supply chain partners will become the link through which the essential processes of managing and synchronising supply chains are carried out.

2.20 The linking of systems has become necessary because of customers' ever increasing demands. Customers are looking beyond cost as the sole measure of value. They are demanding innovation and personalisation of both products and the associated service and delivery.

11

2.21 Supply chains in all industries are meeting with new requirements for competition in the e-business environment, characterised by mass customisation, massive scalability, faster and more flexible fulfilment, and the ability to develop new channels that attract and serve larger customer bases.

2.22 Traditional supply chain initiatives alone, such as strategic sourcing and joint product development, do not sufficiently prepare organisations for e-business competition. The traditional supply chain means establishing long-term relationships with vendors, distributors and retailers, with multiple inventory sites, long lead-times and fixed margins.

2.23 This traditional approach will no longer be enough to compete. Shrinking product lifecycles require partnership with customers and a broader range of suppliers to better customise product to those customers' demands in substantially reduced time-to-market periods.

2.24 The message of the internet-enabled supply chain is that the internet will not replace supply chain management. Rather, it is a tool that allows supply chain activities to be carried out in a synchronised fashion. Internet-enabled tools and solutions allow development of cost efficient, service effective supply chains. However, speed is the key capability that defines the new supply chain in the internet age.

3   Electronic catalogues

Electronic catalogues (e-catalogues) and directory listings

3.1 E-catalogues and directories are used in many e-marketplaces and can also be accessible directly on the internet, providing searchable databases of information about suppliers, products and services. Some e-marketplaces offer a directory of suppliers listed by products or services provided, with links to supplier websites.

3.2 Some e-marketplaces provide a single catalogue of all suppliers and products, while others have links to individual supplier catalogues. With e-marketplace catalogues, customers can research a wide range of products and suppliers from a central source. They can then buy in one transaction from a single site.

3.3 Catalogues are important to companies for marketing purposes because they are one of the main ways to distribute product information to public marketplaces and private exchanges.

3.4 A catalogue can be defined as 'a complete enumeration of items arranged systematically with descriptive details'. An e-catalogue is an electronic document which carries the product specifications, listings and information in detail. Successful catalogue management improves the working relationship between customers and supplier. It also automatically provides a passage to sourced products, suppliers and the ordering process. Catalogues also provide a link to product reviews and other relevant industry information.

3.5 Catalogue content is not restricted to listings of product details. It also helps in many other ways.

- Helping the supplier in creating, analysing and validating catalogue content
- Driving, monitoring and maintaining communication between all the involved parties
- Performing content validation against data formats, business logic and coding structures
- Monitoring all catalogue management processes
- Updating the list at the instant a new product is in the market by making it available for the customer

- Providing comparison of product features, advising on related products and alternative products, and on services to customers

3.6 E-catalogues can suffer from excessive information. The reasoning behind using an e-marketplace or going direct with an e-directory is the management behind the catalogue. An effective e-catalogue should be able to carry out several core functions.

- It must support a search for a list of products that meet some set of buyer-defined search criteria. Additionally, the catalogue needs to be smart enough to return only items that the buyer is authorised to see.
- It must provide more detailed product information after the search returns a set of candidate products: additional product specifications, a description of value-added services or perhaps a picture.
- It must be a link between the catalogue item, and more dynamic information: inventory availability information that will vary over time, delivery specifications, contract specific terms and conditions, and pricing information that will vary for each customer.
- It must address the full lifecycle, from creation and authoring to search and interaction with external systems, including routine maintenance of the item descriptions and attributes.
- Although the type of additional product information will vary by industry, supplier and class of goods, the catalogue must always provide enough information for a buyer to make an unassisted decision.

Benefits of using e-catalogues

3.7 Handling a paper catalogue is tiring and tedious. It consumes lots of space and time and is also expensive to produce. Online catalogues can be easily updated, are designed to be easily searchable, and can be accessed at the click of a button.

3.8 Purchases are made by selecting items from the catalogue. The online system gives the supplier the opportunity to receive the purchase orders online which will lead to cost savings and more straightforward administration. The system helps in the accuracy of the orders placed as it reduces the time which was previously used to confirm the quotes and prices by presenting the product details and specifications in full length.

3.9 Accurately showcased online catalogues can reduce the error rate of mismatches between the invoice and the purchase order.

4 The use of technology to exchange data

Integrating systems along the supply chain

4.1 The traditional view of the purchasing cycle has been impacted heavily over recent years by new technology. One area that has seen considerable growth is the integration of systems among organisations.

4.2 Any business that has invested in technology over a period of years is likely to find itself with a number of different systems and software programs that may prove incompatible with each other over time. The order process system may not talk to the accounts software, the forecasting system may not link to the purchasing system, and so on. Systems can in many ways hinder as well as support business objectives.

4.3   Larger organisations have been able to view IT differently. Many have looked at installing and supporting an enterprise resource planning system (ERP) since they were first developed in the mid 1990s. These systems provide an integrated approach to all the component parts of an organisation's business.

4.4   ERP systems have also been important in the integration of IT systems *between* organisations. With investment by the major hardware and software developers linked to the rapid growth of IT capability what seemed unlikely ten years ago is now a reality for many small and medium sized enterprises – the ability to integrate systems between organisations. Specialist systems integration companies now provide services to meet the needs of smaller organisations.

The benefits

4.5   The concept behind integration is simple: the whole can be greater than the sum of the parts. The more systems and processes link together, the greater the overall benefit.

4.6   Integrated systems are viewed as more agile and responsive in the way they operate. Linking with other companies or bodies allows them to streamline their operation by improving the flow of information between companies, meeting the needs of companies they interlink with and often being viewed as a business partner over the long term.

4.7   Here are some of the principal benefits.

- Improved efficiency. Integrated systems give greater accuracy and reduce waste as they allow organisations to operate using real-time figures rather than estimates. Production can be linked to ordering; purchasing can be linked to finance; and so on.
- Improved job satisfaction. Staff morale improves as integration reduces administration and allows staff to focus on the more skilled aspects of their job. Linked systems benefit as information is better, reducing frustration and helping to improve work-rates.
- Competitive advantage. Integration places an organisation in a strong position to improve relationships with customers and suppliers. Many businesses will collaborate on forecasts and purchasing with suppliers, or give customers direct access to certain levels of their systems. In turn other companies will reciprocate by allowing similar interrogation of their systems.

Integration options

4.8   Organisations looking to integrate systems need to decide on the best approach for them and their future business needs. This section examines some of the technical solutions available.

4.9   An **integration hub** is a method of linking processes and systems gradually. In essence it is a system that sits between existing systems and enables them to talk to one another. This comes from the fact that many organisations have developed IT systems in a piecemeal manner, making the best decisions at the time but perhaps failing to consider the future needs of the business. As an example, accounting packages such as Sage can be integrated with orders, purchasing and stock demands.

4.10   The benefit of an integration hub is that there is no requirement to replace all the existing systems. Some hubs use XML (extensible mark-up language) as a way of formatting data which then allows information to be shared across different platforms and across the web.

4.11   A **hosted solution** allows you to rent integration services over the internet from application service providers (ASPs). The software is hosted and maintained by the ASP as a form of outsourcing. This approach can be seen as more flexible than an integration hub, with support and upgrades forming an integral part of the contract. As with any outsourced contract you will be heavily reliant on the provider which may prove problematic if you decide to end the contract.

4.12 **Systems integrators** are individuals or businesses that build computing systems for clients by combining hardware and software products from multiple vendors. Using a systems integrator, a company can align cheaper, pre-configured components and off-the-shelf software to meet key business goals, as opposed to more expensive, customised implementations that may require original programming or manufacture of unique components. Creation of these information systems may include designing or building customised architecture, integrating it with new or existing hardware, packaged and custom software, and communications infrastructure.

4.13 **Solutions providers** are the big software players such as SAP and Oracle that build bespoke integration solutions based on their own proprietary software. With their own software widely accepted across the industry this solution is highly suitable for those organisations wishing to develop a fully integrated system with the ability to be controlled and maintained in house.

4.14 This provides a powerful, industry-standard, robust solution but comes at a high price. Solutions providers have tended to be used by blue chip companies and larger organisations but new products have been developed over recent years that now makes this option more attractive to the SME sector.

Electronic data interchange

4.15 Electronic data interchange (EDI) is the use of computer and telecommunications technology to move data between or within organisations in a structured data format that permits information to be transferred from a computer program in one location to a computer program in another location, without manual intervention.

4.16 An example is the transmission of an electronic invoice from a supplier's invoicing software to a customer's accounts receivable software. This definition includes the direct transmission of data between locations, transmission using an intermediary such as a communication network, and the exchange of digital storage devices such as magnetic tapes and CD-ROMs.

4.17 EDI is one of the most important aspects of electronic commerce enabling the information exchange between two parties in a commercial transaction. The intent of all electronic commerce is to automate business processes. Some transactions can be completely paperless and move data from one computer application to another computer application. EDI falls under this type of electronic commerce.

4.18 EDI is commonly defined as 'the direct computer-to-computer exchange of standard business forms'. The key idea involved is the exchange of documents that allow a business application to take place without human intervention. Data communication is then necessary for the exchange to take place.

4.19 Many businesses choose EDI as a fast, inexpensive, and safe method of sending purchase orders, requests for quotations, quotations, invoices, payments, and other frequently used business documents.

11

The business process and EDI

4.20 Any business application that can be improved through paperless trading in a fast, efficient environment is a good candidate for EDI. EDI is currently widely used by the airline industry, banking industry, credit card industry, and auto industry. The current push in the EDI world comes from companies who wish to trade with each other electronically, particularly buyers and their suppliers.

4.21 The traditional document flow for purchasing transactions starts with data entry by the purchaser to create a paper document to send by mail to trading partners. Once the trading partners receive the data, they keystroke the information received into a local application and then perform more data entry by entering a response into a local application. The resultant paper document is then mailed to the purchaser.

4.22 The procedure is both time consuming and labour intensive because data from both trading partners has to be entered twice, once at the point of creation and once at the point of entry to the foreign system. In addition, the originator must await a paper response sent by mail.

4.23 EDI data is keyed in only once, at the original point of entry. The data is then translated into a standard format electronically and sent to the trading partner electronically. At the receiving end, the data fields are mapped into local applications, and the only data entry required is for new data that may be needed to respond to the data received.

The benefits of EDI

4.24 The amount of value to be gained from EDI implementation depends on whether or not it is integrated into the overall data processing effort of the organisation. The effects of EDI depend greatly on the level of automation within an organisation.

4.25 The list of EDI-related benefits – lower costs, higher productivity, and reduced order-cycle times – is attainable, but if the automation level of the organisation is not high and is not integrated, the benefits of EDI will be lessened considerably.

4.26 EDI is well established as effective technology for reducing costs and increasing efficiency.

Value-added networks (VANs)

4.27 Setting up to use EDI involves considerable expense and for small businesses, and businesses that do low volumes between each other, the cost is not always worth the efficiencies achieved. Commercial value-added networks (VANs) simplify exchange of data by offering their communications services to prospective EDI users.

4.28 VANs establish communications paths between their customers and with other VANs. By using these services a business does not have to worry about the many communications complexities from having trading partners using different hardware, software, and transport mechanisms.

4.29 Mailbox software is the most important feature offered by VANs. The electronic mailbox is used for both store-and-retrieve and store-and-forward operations. In both cases, the sender of the EDI message transmits the electronic message to the VAN on its own time schedule. The VAN then acts on the message depending on whether the service is store-and-retrieve or store-and-forward.

- Store-and-retrieve service allows the VAN to store the message in the receiver's mail box. The receiver then retrieves its messages based upon the needs and schedules of the receiver. This service enables the sender and receiver to communicate, but at different times of the day, instead of simultaneously.
- Store-and-forward service allows the VAN to forward messages to the receiver when the business need is not for immediate or event-driven notification. Event-driven mailbox services can be handled by forwarding of the message to the receiver or by immediate notification from the VAN to the receiver that a message has been stored that meets the prearranged criteria for event-driven notification.

> ## Chapter summary
>
> - A supply chain is a network of retailers, distributors, transporters, storage facilities and suppliers that participate in the production, delivery and sale of a product to the customer.
> - Nowadays, management of supply chains is heavily dependent on information technology.
> - An intranet is a private internal business network that enables companies to share information, to collaborate and to improve their communications. An extranet is an extension of this concept: it allows external organisations (eg suppliers) to access selected areas of the intranet.
> - Buyers rely increasingly on electronic catalogues and directories.
> - Increasingly, organisations seek to integrate their own information systems with those of other organisations in the supply chain.
> - One well developed example of systems integration is electronic data interchange (EDI).

Self-test questions

Numbers in brackets refer to paragraphs where you can check your answers.

1   List three key elements making up a supply chain. (1.2)

2   List important questions to be answered in designing a supply chain. (1.7)

3   Explain how an intranet works. (2.4)

4   List possible contents of an intranet. (2.8)

5   How can an intranet improve business efficiency? (2.11)

6   In what ways can electronic catalogues assist buyers? (3.5)

7   What are the main benefits of integrating information systems along a supply chain? (4.7)

8   Explain how EDI works. (4.15ff)